AF505599

International Political Economy Series
Series Standing Order ISBN 0–333–71708–2
(outside North America only)

You can receive future titles in this series as they are published by placing a standing order.
Please contact your bookseller or, in case of difficulty, write to us at the address below with
your name and address, the title of the series and the ISBN quoted above.

Customer Services Department, Macmillan Distribution Ltd, Houndmills, Basingstoke,
Hampshire RG21 6XS, England

Regionalization and Security in Southern Africa

Nana Poku
Senior UN Researcher and Lecturer
Southampton University

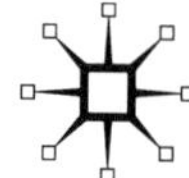

First published 2001 by
PALGRAVE
Houndmills, Basingstoke, Hampshire RG21 6XS and
175 Fifth Avenue, New York, N. Y. 10010
Companies and representatives throughout the world

PALGRAVE is the new global academic imprint of
St. Martin's Press LLC Scholarly and Reference Division and
Palgrave Publishers Ltd (formerly Macmillan Press Ltd).

ISBN 0–333–74844–1

This book is printed on paper suitable for recycling and made from fully managed and sustained forest sources.

A catalogue record for this book is available from the British Library.

Library of Congress Cataloging-in-Publication Data
Poku, Nana, 1971–
    Regionalization and security in Southern Africa / Nina [i.e. Nana] Poku.
       p. cm. — (International political economy series)
    Includes bibliographical references and index.
    ISBN 0–333–74844–1 (cloth)
    1. Africa, Southern—Economic integration. 2. Africa, Southern–
    –Dependency on foreign countries. 3. Africa, Southern—Economic
    conditions. 4. Security, International. I. Title. II. Series.
    HC900 .P65 2000
    337.1'6—dc21

                                                        00–040461

10   9   8   7   6   5   4   3   2   1
10   09   08   07   06   05   04   03   02   01

Printed and bound in Great Britain by
Antony Rowe Ltd, Chippenham, Wiltshire

To
Professor Stephen Chan

For his contribution to the study of Africa's International Relations

Contents

List of Tables

Acknowledgements

Whatever the weaknesses of this project, they would have been far greater without the kind help of key friends. In this context, many thanks and gratitude to Stephen Chan, Peter Vale, Neil Renwick, Wayne Edge, Richard Calland, Jacqui Lewin and Yan Fa Li. I am particularly grateful to Juliet McBride for her encouragement.

I am most beholden to everyone who took an interest in the project, but special thanks must go to Aruna Vasudevan – my commissioning editor at Macmillan – for her patience and support and also to Anne Rafique for making my work readable.

What follows is, of course, my own responsibility.

N.P.

Abbreviations and Acronyms

AAM	Anti-Apartheid Movement (England)
ACP	African, Caribbean and Pacific countries, signatories to the Lomé Conventions
ADB	African Development Bank
AEC	African Economic Community
ANC	African National Congress
APEC	Asia Pacific Economic Cooperation
ASEAN	Association of South East Asian Nations
BLSN	Botswana, Lesotho, Swaziland and Namibia
BLS	Botswana, Lesotho and Swaziland
CABEI	Central American Bank for Economic Integration
CACM	Central American Common Market Association
CCA	Common customs area
CEAO	Communauté Economiqué de l'Afrique de l'Ouest
CMA	Common monetary area
CODESA	Convention for a Democratic South Africa
COMESA	Common Market for Eastern and Southern Africa
CONSAS	Constellation of Southern African States
COSATU	Congress of South African Trade Unions
CSS	Central Statistics Service
DAC	Development Assistance Committee (of the OECD)
DBSA	Development Bank of Southern Africa
EAC	East African Community
EACM	East African Common Market
EC	European Community
ECA	Economic Commission for Africa
ECLA	Economic Commission for Latin America
ECM	European Common Market
ECOWAS	Economic Community of West African States
ECSC	European Coal and Steel Community
EEA	European Economic Area
EFTA	European Free Trade Area
EPG	European Planning Group
ESADB	Eastern and Southern African Development Bank

EU	European Union
FRELIMO	Frente de Libertação de Moçambique
FTA	Free Trade Area
GATT	General Agreement on Tariffs and Trade
GDP	Gross Domestic Product
GEAR	Growth Employment and Redistribution Policy
GNP	Gross National Product
GSM	Generalized System of Preferences
HIPC	Heavily Indebted Poor Country
IBRD	International Bank for Reconstruction and Development
IDA	International Development Assistance
IFI	International financial institution
ILO	International Labour Organization
IMF	International Monetary Fund
LAFTA	Latin American Free Trade Association
LAIA	Latin American Integration Association
LAND	Lesotho National Development Corporation
LCD	Less developed country
MDC	More developed country
MFN	Most favoured nation
MPLA	Movement Popular de Libertação de Angola
NAFTA	North American Free Trade Area
NGO	Non-governmental organization
NIC	Newly industrialized country
OAU	Organization of African Unity
ODA	Official Development Assistance
OECD	Organization for Economic Cooperation and Development
OPEC	Organization of Petroleum Exporting Countries
PAC	Pan-African Congress
PTA	Preferential Trade Area for Eastern and Southern Africa
RDP	Reconstruction and Development Programme
RENAMO	Resistência Nacional de Moçambique
RIA	Regional integration agreements
RMA	Rand Monetary Area
SACU	Southern African Customs Union
SADC	Southern African Development Community
SADCC	Southern African Development Coordination Conference
SAIIA	Southern African Institute of International Affairs

SAP	Structural Adjustment Programme
SAR	Southern African Region
SARB	South African Reserve Bank
SATS	South African Transport Systems
SEA	Single European Act
SSA	Sub-Saharan Africa
SWAPO	South West African People's Organisation
TINET	PTA Programme for Trade Information
TNC	Transnational Corporation
UAPTA	PTA Unit of Account
UDF	United Democratic Front
UN	United Nations
UNCTAD	United Nations Conference on Trade and Development
UNESCO	United Nations Education, Science and Cultural Organization
UNICEF	United Nations Childrens Fund
UNIDO	United Nations Industrial Development Organization
UNITA	União Nacional para Independência Total de Angola
WTO	World Trade Organization

Introduction

Relations among southern African states are more cordial than at any time in recent memory.[1] Government officials, business leaders and academic scholars have been gathering with increasing frequency in regional capitals to discuss problems of regional concerns and to search for institutional frameworks for joint action. As the region enters the new millennium, states are developing increasingly active and dense networks of private as well as public ties that bind them together in an interdependent economic, political and cultural system. The rising volume of trade flows, cross-border investments, interlocking financial deals, diplomatic consultations, cultural exchanges and tourism manifests these ties. Moreover, visible progress is being made to resolve past conflicts such as those in Mozambique, Angola and South Africa.[2]

Collectively, these changes are being viewed by many as steps towards a wider regional political and economic accommodation offering the prospect of regional economic renewal driven by the 'powerhouse' of the South African economy.[3] On this view, the southern African economies, hitherto constrained by the destructive and divisive economic dependence on apartheid South Africa, are now on course for an era of natural, constructive and cooperative economic 'interdependence'.[4] Central to this optimism is a series of assumptions about South Africa and its future role in the region. The transition within the country is expected to be relatively straightforward: the 'old' South Africa was destabilizing for the region, and the 'new' South Africa will therefore be an unmitigated good for the entire subcontinent.[5] This view emphasizes the need for regional developments to be based on qualitative transformation of existing relations. Central here is the assumption that regional and other relations need to be restructured as an integral part of a process of transforming the existing growth path. 'Intersecting concrete needs and interests make it possible', in Robert Davies' view, 'to envisage a mutually beneficial, negotiated restructuring of regional economic relations which will address several of the key problems of the inequality and longer-term unsustainability of existing relations.'[6]

This would be centred on a trade-off in which South Africa would be expected to grant greater access to regional markets and inputs in return for cooperating with the region in restructuring key sector relations. These would include: granting regional states greater access to the domestic South African market; accepting the need to grant favourable terms to regional suppliers of inputs like water and hydropower; participating in the process of restructuring regional transport relations; committing itself to finding mutually acceptable regional solutions to problems arising from labour migration; and investigating the possibilities for a mineral-based regional industrialization strategy.[7] It would also involve some process of negotiating new regional relations, a programme of institutional reform and development, and an equitable and mutually beneficial pattern of new regional relations.[8]

In short, South Africa is expected to shoulder the costs of initiating economic development in one of the world's poorest regions. Implicit in this view is a particular conception of the notion of 'public goods'. In this context, 'public goods' describes regional benefits that can be shared non-competitively. Specifically, the benefits from the 'public goods' would have two characteristics: first, they would be non-divisible in the sense that their consumption by one state would not reduce their consumption by another state. Second, they would be non-excludable in the sense that once these goods are provided to any state, it is impossible or very costly to prevent others from enjoying them. Regional peace, stability and order are the public goods which South Africa would be expected to guarantee. On the assumption that South Africa is sufficiently wealthy and powerful to afford a disproportionate amount of the costs for supplying these public goods, it also likely to have the motivation for doing so. That is, as the wealthiest and most powerful regional state, it has the greatest vested interest in preserving stability and encouraging economic growth in the region. It follows, therefore, that even though South Africa has to pay more than others (at least, at the beginning), its benefits from the public goods would still be greater than its costs. In other words, even though the burden of providing the public goods will proportionately fall on the hegemon (in the most extreme cases, the hegemon may assume the entire costs of the public good), it still is absolutely better off with the provision than without the provision of these public goods.

The vast majority of the empirical support for this thesis is drawn from a particular reading of the role played by the United States after the Second World War. In the work of, among others, Robert Gilpin, Robert Keohane and Charles Kindleberger, a positive picture is often painted of the United States emerging out of the Second World War with unrivalled power, prestige and political purpose. According to this picture, in an attempt to contain communism, the United States constructed a politico-economic order to safeguard the western democratic alliance against the Soviet Union (and also China). During this period, the US international role was considerable. It was the leading member and host government for the premier intergovernmental organization, the United Nations. Moreover, the United States exercised a decisive voice in the formation and evolution of various international monetary and trade agreements. The Bretton Woods multilateral accord (1947) provided for a system of fixed exchange rates (within 1 per cent of their value pegged to gold). To provide international monetary stability and liquidity, the US government committed itself to convert dollars into gold, thereby making the US dollar the international currency of choice (the convertibility of dollars into gold was withdrawn in 1971).

The United States also took a leading role in formulating the new international commercial order after the Second World War. The result was the creation of the General Agreement on Tariffs and Trade (now the World Trade Organization – WTO). This agreement codified the prevailing consensus on free trade and banned discriminatory commercial practices as well as unilateral trade quotas. GATT laid the foundation for the progressive liberalization of international trade (such as by encouraging the reduction of tariffs and extension of trade advantages equally to all members of GATT through the most-favoured-nation clause) in the subsequent two and a half decades. Together these institutions are said to have provided public goods in the form of ensuring international peace, deterring military aggression, promoting monetary stability and encouraging free trade.[9] The other western countries were in effect permitted a free ride. That is, they were allowed to pay less than their proportionate share of the costs for these public goods. This, in turn, enabled them to grow at a faster rate than they ordinarily would have and the longer-term result has been the prosperity and relative stability currently evident in the global political economy.[10]

Is South Africa really in a position to play such a role in the development of southern Africa? Can it afford to balance domestic expectations with the need to develop the region? Moreover, will regional states legitimate South Africa's dominance by endorsing its leadership? The cultural and economic diversity of the regional states has resulted in a position where regional consciousness does not currently exist, and because of the great disparities in industrial maturity, fears of economic exploitation abound. Just as there are still widespread concerns in Western Europe about a resurgent Germany and in the Pacific region about Japan, South Africa's neighbours have not forgotten the country's recent dark history. Those memories are still vivid in the minds of many regional policy-makers and civilians who obviously would not welcome a renewed South African dominance in any form in the new regional order. This means that any project which seeks to confirm South African hegemony will have to grapple with the real legacy of apartheid, the fear of South African dominance, and the real or perceived interests of individual states.

Predicated on the region's turbulent history, this book seeks to outline the contours of the emerging politico-economic order. Naturally, it would be impossible to compress a discussion of the entire complex and evolving reality of the subcontinent into a relatively small book. As a result, I have been somewhat eclectic in borrowing various perspectives from such social science disciplines as sociology, economics, history and political science. Concomitantly, I try to address audiences in both international relations and comparative politics, while keeping the book within the page limits of a supplementary text. These multiple goals have naturally forced some compromises. Thus I have attempted to highlight major analytical distinctions rather than to dwell on subtle historical nuances. Some countries and topics are de-emphasized and even bypassed in favour of others. My intention is not to offer a text on physical or cultural geography, nor do I intend to provide country specific accounts of recent developments. Rather, I hope to apply certain contemporary social science perspectives and concepts to the southern African context in order to illuminate some salient policy problems and empirical patterns suggested by recent developments. A conscientious effort is therefore made to balance historical description with analytical explanations.

Analytical and theoretical framework

In the past such an undertaking would have been dominated by the analytical insights of the modernization/diffusionist and dependency paradigms. Both the dependency and modernization frameworks were based on a sense of determinism or fatalism. That is, pre-specified outcomes were associated with the development process with little or no attempt to examine the spatial and temporal contingencies of development. The conceptual flaws inherent in these theoretical constructions are aptly summarized by Lipietz:

> Despite the undeniable formal superiority of the imperialism-dependency approach, it seems that, like the rival liberal approach, it had degenerated into an ahistoric dogmatism . . . It is as though the two theories were contemplating the development of history . . . if the South was stagnating, one theorist would tell you precisely what time it was; if new industrialisation was taking place, another would say I told you so . . . [11]

In the southern African context the dependency/modernization thesis gave rise to two developments. The first is that the regional economy came to be viewed solely from the perspective of South African hegemony. In other words, the region's economic ties were evaluated in terms of how they strengthened the South African state. There were no considerations given to how these ties might weaken the regime; equally, there was no consideration given to how they might strengthen other states in the region. The odious nature of apartheid, it appears, was sufficient to discourage scholars and commentators from investigating the positive side of southern African economic relations with South Africa. In general these ties were solely regarded as being detrimental to their developmental goals by opening regional states up to intimidation, pressure and blackmail by South Africa. Hence, regional organizations such as the SADC, PTA and OAU among others became preoccupied with utopian strategies and plans for 'disengaging' southern African states from their ties with South Africa and with visionary proposals for creating *de novo* a new regional economy that excluded the pariah state.

As a result, political analysis of southern Africa was largely under-developed. What discussions there were, were reduced to cataloguing economic relationships between South Africa and other states in the region. Inevitably authors would note that the particular relationship under discussion was asymmetrical and that South Africa could more easily forgo the benefits derived from the relationship than could its partners. From that it was inferred that South Africa derived political leverage or power over other states in the region.[12] An indication of the inadequacy of this approach is the fact that despite revolutionary political change in the region since 1974 writers have continued to observe the same asymmetrical relationships with South Africa and have arrived at the same conclusion regarding South Africa's domination of the region.

While this suggests a remarkable continuity of regional economic networks, the observation contributes little to an explanation of the profound political changes occurring in the region. This indicates either that an understanding of the region's economic ties contributes little to our understanding of political changes within regions or, as seems more likely, suggests an underdeveloped political analysis of socio-economic relationships. Indeed, a wide range of often conflicting state actions is attributed to these asymmetrical relationships without any political analysis at all. In the case of the Southern African Customs Union (SACU), for example, Botswana, Lesotho and Swaziland are treated in the literature as if they are so completely dependent upon the South African economy that politically they are 'hostage' states. This is attributed to the fact that they are geographically encompassed by South Africa, they lack resources and they need to export labour to South Africa. The prevailing view is that these governments could not survive a disruption of their economic relations with South Africa. The implication is that they also could not afford to challenge the South African political regime. The difficulty here is that the logic is based upon the assumption that South Africa is able to use its economic ties with these countries as political leverage over them. This conclusion, however, tends to 'ignore how domestic political forces constrain economic policy and shape state responses to the external environment'.[13]

One way to overcome this dilemma is to consider the advice given by Lipietz that we obviously have to take into account the historical and national diversity of capital accumulation in each country under consideration.[14] This, of course, is very similar to recent calls from John Ruggie and Robert Cox to bring socio-economic factors into the analysis of international relations. Ruggie draws attention to the linkages of property rights and capitalism to political sovereignty, while Cox wants to include the social forces engendered by the organization of production.[15] Thus, rather than emphasizing unicausal parsimony in conformity, they rightly pose a constructivist view by arguing that a complex array of social forces crucially condition any set of outcomes and that any event or series of events emerges out of the totality of social life.[16]

How might this formulation be spelled out and, in turn, related to research on southern Africa?[17] In the first instance, constructivists do not deny the existence of an independent phenomenal world. Indeed, they insist that each datum remains an intersubjectively discriminable aspect of the world. However, they do contend that we can never know all the features of the world independent of the discourses about it. As Onuf has succinctly noted, we 'construct worlds we know in a world we do not'.[18] Accordingly, constructivists view the relationship between the subject and the social world as radically unstable and variable, and refuse to grant sovereignty to either. On this basis, Onuf has argued for a conception of world politics which regards human subjects and societies as, quite simply, constructing or constituting each other. From this perspective, poststructuralists are right to deconstruct the constitution of the subject in modernity and reject the subject/object dichotomy, but wrong not to simply transcend the duality. We do not have to accept that we are either within or outside history, for 'we are always within our constructions even as we choose to stand apart from them, condemn them, or reconstruct them'.[19]

The constructivist thus has it both ways, positing a foundation that the act of constitution (the co-constitution of people and society) makes history, while also asserting that social construction is 'a contingent effect of political practices within history'.[20] Such a claim can also be conceived as part of a wider effort to transcend the dichotomy between objectivism and relativism in contemporary social theory by developing a notion of human rationality as practical but critical reason or wisdom.[21] By rejecting the subject/object dichotomy and embedding the analyst, and indeed all human agents and subjects, in the co-constitution of history, constructivism opens up a rapprochement between philosophy and ontology or theories about the making of social worlds and histories, and with these the making of being-in-the-world.

Orthodox (positivist) views of ontology define it as consisting of 'things' and 'entities', and the relationships between them, imputed to the real world and invoked in a theory, research programme or discourse's explanations. A constructivist, by contrast, emphasizes the plurality of the social worlds human agents create (or, in the jargon, co-constitute) notwithstanding the existence of an independent phenomenal world. This then brings us to consider what an adequate social ontology would look like. One approach would point to the pervasive role of rules in bounding (although not governing) human conduct. This suggests a particular agent-structure or structurationist claim with regard to ontology where structure is understood as generative of rules and resources. Significantly, recent work in social theory suggests the terms of a 'structurationist' claim in which action and structure are regarded as the complementary terms of a duality: the 'duality of structure'.[22]

This notion, advanced by the leading exponent of 'structurationism', Anthony Giddens, conceives structure as both the medium and the outcome of the conduct it recursively (backwardly) organizes.[23] It suggests that the structures which render an action possible are, in the performance of the action, reconstituted. It also suggests that 'structures' (or more precisely, the structural properties of social life) do not exist outside action, for it is only through the practices of agents that they are instantiated, reproduced and, potentially, transformed.[24] Agents, in Giddens' schema, are knowledgeable in that they are capable of both rationalizing their actions and reflexively monitoring their locale and context through time. They enjoy discursive consciousness, and a wider 'practical consciousness' of things known and understood about the world without being articulated as such. They also choose whether to follow a rule or not in the light of their assessment of the consequences of such conduct. More generally,

Giddens affirms the centrality of agents when he emphasizes that it is their very reflexivity which opens up the possibility of multiple motivations and interpretations of any situation, and with this the agent's ability to 'act otherwise' whether the specific agent is advantaged or disadvantaged in resource terms.[25]

This argument as to the transformative capability of agency and the possibility of doing 'otherwise' is the first face of power in 'structurationism'. Although we might suspect this represents a slide to voluntarism, Giddens contends not: he accepts a notion of structural constraint defined broadly as the setting of limits upon the feasible range of choices that an actor can follow. He also seeks not to equate social structure with practical knowledge and hence elides the distinction between an analysis of the structural conditions of a certain kind of society, and a mere summary of what actors already know in 'knowing how to go on' in that society. The accounts agents are able to give of their actions, Giddens contends, are 'bounded' by both the unintended consequences of action and the unacknowledged conditions of action. The latter subsumes the former in so far as the unintended consequence of action is the reproduction of a structural property which renders further action possible. The inherent reflexivity of agents and the role of social science in elucidating structural conditions merely create the possibility of intentionally transforming practices, institutions and structural constraints.

It follows from this discussion that while the structural properties of social life are constituted and reconstituted by agents they are also constitutive of them in that they form sets of relations that 'mobilize bias' and help define the identities, powers and interests of agents that occupy social structural positions. A reference to 'social structural positions' is, however, somewhat misleading for Giddens deems structures to have no descriptive qualities of their own in that they exist only as memory traces and as the instantiation of rules in the situated activities and practices of agents. Rather, 'structure' represents 'materials' in the form of rules and resources drawn upon and reproduced in action. For this reason, Giddens generically defines structure as generative rules and resources. Power in this context is defined not as a resource but as a distinct type of organizational power or generalized means drawn upon in action. Different types of social (organizational) power and knowledgeability generate particular logistical techniques, which, in turn, are promiscuous in the sense that no one social group permanently controls such techniques. Giddens shares this 'organizational' or 'institutionalist' conception of power with other historical sociologists such as Mann.[26]

To theorize the scope for change in both time and space raises important questions about the purpose of political inquiry and its relationship to political practice. As we noted in the introduction, established research into southern Africa tends to aim for predictive power, social control and order. These aims are both problematic in principle and elusive in practice. In the first instance, most empirical work about the region has been premised on positivist/empiricist theories of knowledge, and for this reason have been vulnerable to the argument that they legitimate the interests and social forces they merely purport to describe. Such claims are reinforced to the extent that work like Laurie Nathan's *The Changing of the Guard* or Pierre du Toit's *State Building and Democracy in Southern Africa*, emphasize constraint and necessity in regional affairs without theorizing the multiple sources of change in social life and the scope these imply for achieving ethical norms which are both desirable and possible in regional affairs. By contrast, highlighting the co-constructed or constituted character of both research and social life (the so-called 'ontological turn' in social theory) yields a quite different appreciation of the links between knowledge, action and power, and, in turn, the plurality of possible social worlds.

Constructivism, drawing on the insights of philosophical and historical hermeneutics, captures the way inquiry is initially directed by research traditions and prejudgements, and then openly risked in the attempt to understand other texts, traditions and forms of life. In this pursuit of understanding, intellectual horizons are challenged and prone to change. This, in turn, suggests the links to praxis and moral-practical knowledge integral to research and social understanding: the interlacing of views of authority and tradition with the 'objects' or topics of inquiry and our future-oriented views of the world. The co-constituted character of both understanding and social life also implies that social realities are not fixed and therefore necessarily controllable in predictable ways. Policy-makers, for instance, may absorb and act on the findings of social research and thereby transform social rules and 'reality'. This unstable nexus between analysts and policy-makers is a classic instance of the so-called 'double hermeneutic' where theories that begin as strictly explanatory accounts are appropriated by the agents under study and become constitutive of the realm of activity.

In sum, then, it is argued that a constructivist epistemology and a structurationist ontology linked to claims of complexity and historicity provide a more adequate appreciation of the links between knowledge and power. They challenge conventional notions of necessity and clearly legitimate the role of intentional conduct to change constitutive and constraining rules by knowledgeable, reflexive agents reconsidering history in the light of different traditions of understanding. For this reason Dessler describes a structurationist ontology as a 'transformational' model. On this view, structurationism can be said to inform at least certain variants of critical social theory and, in turn, a so-called emancipatory interest in knowledge: an interest in understanding the socially generated impediments to human freedom and autonomy.[27] A generation of these forms of knowledge is central to a fuller understanding of the emerging regional order in southern Africa.

Research in this vein aims not merely to list developments but to capture their historically specific forms of intersection. There is already evidence of important work being done in this genre. Although this work has, predictably, had less impact on international development and development policy debates, it provides the basis for a theoretically informed historical perspective on 'development' which is global in its level of analysis. This work has sought to privilege the specific over the systemic. Dissatisfaction with the elite-oriented focus of much of the work on India, for example, has given rise to Subaltern Studies. Informed by Gramscian, and later poststructural theory, Subaltern approaches have focused on the peasantry and workers with particular concern to delineate structures and techniques of domination, strategies of resistance and the historical particularity and role of culture and religion. The concern here is to restore the subaltern class to history, and provide the intellectual underpinning for a less elite-orientated politics. In general, these scholars aim to draw attention to the way in which the expanding world economy has neither historically nor currently levelled 'pre-capitalist' structures and discourses to the degree that many of the earlier theoretical models implied.

Again, using Latin America as a critical point of study, Steve J. Stern, for example, has shown how the central dynamics of the region's history since the colonial era has been the various approaches and popular resistance strategies of the inhabitants, the interests of mercantile and political elites (whose 'centres of gravity' were in the Americas) and the world-system. For our purpose, what is interesting is how Stern's methodology draws from Jean-François Bayart's *longue durée* thesis which attempts to historicize 'state' in Africa, rejects the state–society dichotomy and argues that colonial and postcolonial 'states' should be seen as historically rooted in particular social formations rather than regarded as alien institutions. This we might call a historicity claim implying an appreciation of the tension between 'structure' and history in the study of societies while, nonetheless, giving priority to history and, in turn, to the historically constituted character of institutions and their endogeneity.[28] Such a claim contests the goal of general unified theory posited by established approaches to southern African studies, recent efforts to make such analyses more differentiated, conditional and context-specific notwithstanding.[29]

Employing such an approach to the current transformation in southern Africa will allow this project both to draw on the recent trends to blend insights across traditions, and to extend it further on the premise that a claim of complexity, not unicausality, is the preferred starting point of analysis. Such a contention finds ready support in certain quarters of international and comparative political economy[30] and among proponents of critical international theory.[31] Instead of viewing the international system as the determinant of national development, complexity demands that we take a more recursive view by arguing that the global/regional political economy simultaneously shapes and is shaped by the historical trajectories of development within individual nation states. This view holds that external dependency and imperialism can be grasped only after the structure, function and policies of individual states and their domestic political economy are understood. This implies that while national development takes place in a regional/international context, there is a variety of possible combinations of national policies that are available for local political actors to pursue.

Structure of the book

The book is organized into five chapters. The first chapter offers a brief history of southern Africa. It highlights some of the more important legacies of colonialism and apartheid, as well as those left by the armed conflicts in recent times. Chapter 2 focuses on the forces which led to the eventual transformation, and then dismantling, of the apartheid state. The chapter also assesses some of the challenges facing the 'New South Africa'. Chapter 3 highlights the forces of regional integration and its relevance for southern Africa. The chapter begins with a look at the theoretical schools, then moves to offer a critical assessment of their failure and future prospects for success. Chapter 4 then moves to discuss the institutional face of southern Africa by assessing the changing nature of SADC, SACU and COMESA in the 'new' regional order. Chapter 5 highlights the critical security issues facing the region as it enters the twenty-first century. The immediate aims of this chapter are twofold: to explore security from a human perspective, and to illustrate this perspective by drawing upon case material from southern Africa.

1

Southern Africa: Colonialism and its Legacies

Sir Alfred Milner.

Black Africa seems to have suffered more severely from outside intervention than any other part of the world. First came the slave trade, which took away millions and degraded both the people and the land. In the wake of the slave trade came European imperialism. Fostered by both was the imposition of the myth of the 'Dark Continent' with its savage people, awaiting the arrival of European culture, technology and religion.[2]

Africa and the impress of colonialism

The first known European contact with Africans can be traced back quite some centuries prior to the infamous partitioning of 1884. The coast of north-west Africa was contacted in the early 1400s, and systematic coastal exploration continued until the end of the century. Despite the fact that Portugal attempted to keep its seafaring technological secrets, it soon began to spread, as in turn did European contact with Africa. Spain entered the competition by mid-century. English and French adventurers appeared in the last decade of the fifteenth century, and the Dutch joined in a century later. The Danes and the Swedes joined the dash for Africa in the 1640s. As the number of European states operating in Africa increased, the competition between them grew, and each found it desirable to operate from specific territorial bases. As many traders' diaries clearly indicate, the Europeans were in their fortresses at the discretion of the local African people. They could have been dislodged at any time.

As the centuries passed, the slave trade began to dominate European–African relations. Seized in their villages along the West African coastland, these once able-bodied men and women were dragged to slave prisons on the coast itself.[3] By the time of its century-long height (from the eighteenth to the mid nineteenth centuries) thousands of men and women were shipped each year across the Atlantic. According to some statistics, as many as one in seven of all the captives shipped for the Americas was dead before the voyage was over. 'The form of stowage', wrote an eyewitness who was a British naval officer in 1849,

> is that the poor wretch shall be seated on his hams, and the head thrust between the knees, and so close that when one moves the mass must ... because of this stowage, the body of the victims become contracted into the deformity of the position, and some that die during the night, stiffen in an sitting posture; others, who outlive the voyage are crippled for life.[4]

Equally disastrous were the impacts on the social-political order of the many parts of the continent. Some regions were virtually depopulated by continual raiding. Disease spread in the wake of disorganization. Arts and crafts disappeared from some cultures. The commercial and social rape of Africa was in full swing by the middle of the nineteenth century. By the later quarter of the nineteenth century, matters got even worse for the Africans. Motivated by a mix of economic and geopolitical considerations, at the conference of Berlin in 1884 the major European powers (Britain, France, Germany, Belgium and Portugal) finally decided the rules for the partitioning of the political landscape of the African continent.

To the colonizers the strategy was remarkably simple and 'civilized': whenever they occupied a piece of land they could legitimately integrate that territory into their empire. The particular motives for declaring a sphere of influence varied, as Europeans, convinced of their 'civilizing role', the 'truth' of their religion and their right to trade, strove to exploit the African continent. For the Europeans it did become a gigantic 'Risk' game, played with real people and real land. Zanzibar was traded for Heligoland, parts of Northern Nigeria were exchanged for fishing rights off Newfoundland, and Cameroun became Kamerun for a 'free hand in Morocco'. This extension of the European notion of sovereignty brought with it a near total compartmentalization of political space in which there were very few uncolonized areas on the continent. Only 10 per cent of the continent was under direct European control in 1870, but by the end of the century only 10 per cent remained outside it.[5] From the ownership of a landholding through a hierarchy of political administrative areas such as the community, county, state and nation, all pieces knitted together with neither overlap nor extension. By 1914, the political map of Africa was virtually complete. The resulting patterns contained comparable administrative units and clearly defined boundaries.

Within these boundaries, the imperial powers constructed African economies to serve European rather than African interests, and integrated African markets into the global division of labour. The rapid construction of commodity export economies (cash crops and minerals) was undertaken, as exemplified by groundnut, cocoa and palm oil from Nigeria, cocoa and gold from the Gold Coast (now Ghana), cotton from Benin and Burkina Faso; coffee from Kenya, Uganda and Tanzania; and ores from Liberia, Guinea and Sierra Leone. (As will become apparent, this construction of Africa economies and the manner in which they were integrated into the global economy has had a significant impact on postcolonial development.)[6] As large-scale plantations developed and expanded on the continent in order to service the demand for these products, so there was an influx of a significant number of European settlers. These settlers were concentrated heavily on the Eastern and Southern parts of the continent as well as in Algeria, altering the socio-economic and political structures of these regions considerably.[7]

The construction of southern Africa

Before the onset of colonial fever in the 1890s, Europeans had already made substantial inroads into southern Africa. During the first quarter of the nineteenth century, events there were dominated by the expansion of European settlement north-eastwards from the Cape. By the 1880s this stream of settlement was already touching the Limpopo, over a thousand miles into the interior from its base at

Cape Town. Before this date very little was know about the region. The little evidence available seems to paint a negative picture of retrogression. We are led to believe that, in general, the region was economically more underdeveloped, politically more inexperienced and culturally more backward than any of the greater colonies of settlement. After one and a half centuries the colony contained one town worthy of a name and five or six little villages.[8] This position was radically transformed after the discovery of incredible mineral wealth in the region.

As one would expect, the historico-economic development of southern Africa is multifaceted. In the last hundred years, however, the region's history has been more influenced by European colonialism than indigenous factors.[9] In general, this colonial impact evolved in several distinct (though not necessarily independent) stages. The initial stage saw the Portuguese establish footholds along the coasts of present-day Angola and Mozambique, notably during the sixteenth and seventeenth centuries. The second stage witnessed the founding of Cape Town (1652) by the Dutch East India Company, and the growth of the Cape Colony attended by strife with the African population, especially along the eastern frontiers. The third stage began with the permanent occupation of the Cape by the British (1806) and includes the acquisition by Britain of the Colony of Natal. During the period the Boers founded their republics of the South African plateau, and Cecil Rhodes' Pioneer Columns secured the region then known as Zambezia (later Rhodesia and more recently Zimbabwe) for the British Crown.

The fourth stage involves southern Africa's participation in the 'scramble' for the rest of the great continent, as Portugal pushed its still essentially coastal dependencies far into the interior, Germany claimed South West Africa, and the British and the Boers engaged in the Boer War. During this fourth stage, the last quarter of the nineteenth century and the first decade of the twentieth, the main elements of the southern African boundary framework were defined, and the political status of the region's territories was also determined. Conquering Britain merged its victorious Cape and Natal colonies with the vanquished Boer republics into the Union of South Africa.

Although conflict was prevalent, it is fair to acknowledge the fact that the colonial powers often cooperated in order to avoid conflict in the region which would disturb their economic interests. One example of this is the Anglo-German Treaty of 1890, which allowed German access to the Zambezi through the Caprivi Strip but stifled the German dream of '*Mittelafrika*'. Another example is the Anglo-Portuguese Treaty of 1891, permitting telegraph communications between the colonies of Angola and Mozambique but preventing the establishment of a Portuguese land bridge.[10]

When analysing the region's development, the influx of settlers into the colonies must also be taken into consideration. Settlement figures within South Africa by the Dutch, French and British immigrants were far higher than those of surrounding colonies.[11] As a result of the asymmetrical immigration patterns, white settlement into southern African originated mainly from the Cape Colony. As these settlers moved further inland, infrastructure was built to meet their needs, as well as those of the territorial administration and the (mainly) mining industries. The infrastructure tended to be initially connected with its points of origin, the British controlled coastlines of South Africa. The advancement of the railways, financed primarily at British expense, stemmed from a British desire to advance into and colonize more of the interior. In the absence of an efficient domestic infrastructural network, the railways were built to provide a regular service for both passengers and goods. For the service to be economically viable, lines had to be built toward the coast when it became necessary to find an additional port. In an attempt to overcome the constraints placed on the British interior by the coastal colonies of Portugal and Germany, Shepstone wrote to Herbert, the Under-Secretary for Colonial Affairs, 'you have now got the Transvaal ... the Orange Free State must soon follow, but I hope that Delegoa Bay will follow first because it is the natural sea-port of this country, and must be had if possible.'[12] Shepstone continued to support the idea of building a railway from the interior to Delegoa Bay until pressure from settlers in Natal, jealous of possible Delegoan prosperity, forced him to abandon the idea.

Secondary industries and settlements evolved around the mining enterprises of the interior and, together with the infrastructure, ensured sustained colonial development. The British financed the bulk of infrastructural development in the region, with other colonial powers investing relatively little amounts. German entrepreneurs were reluctant to invest in the colonies because of the poor economic return, despite some German government subsidies. The Portuguese, in an attempt to develop the interior, imitated the British lead and chartered companies to 'establish civil and military posts and develop agriculture'. One of the companies was charged with 'constructing railroads, roads and ports, settling Portuguese families, building schools and hospitals, and generally developing the area...(but)... disregarding...the Charter, the Company carried out only the construction necessary for these commercial operations'.[13] Thus Britain, through colonial entrepreneurship and diplomatic persuasion,[14] colonized and developed a greater part of the interior, using the South African Colony as a base for these southern African ventures. Britain perceived the region as a single entity rather than as 'parts making up a whole', as is evident in its dealings with the other colonial powers. This legacy of British imperialism proved extremely important as the age of colonialism drew to a close, a point to which we shall return. For now, however, it is important to return to an earlier theme: namely the construction of the region. Of particular importance here are developments in the last hundred years.

Southern Africa: 1900 to the 1960s

The first half of the twentieth century in southern Africa was one of adjustment and colonial accommodation. Major developments included not only the formation of a Union in South Africa, but also the termination of German administration in South West Africa and the establishment there of a South African Mandate under the League of Nations auspices, and the formation, following lengthy preparations, of a Federation in Rhodesia and Nyasaland, as well as the elevation of the Portuguese dependencies to Provinces of the Portuguese state. Even before the Boer War ended, voices had been raised in Britain in opposition to London's campaign, which included concentration camps and a scorched earth policy. Britain's Liberal Party even then committed itself to the restoration of Boer rights in South Africa in the event of its assumption of power. When, in 1905, that party was indeed elected to office, the promise was kept.

British Prime Minister Campbell-Bannerman's objective was far-reaching: he wanted to unite the vanquished high veld republics with the British colonies on the coast in order to create a Union of South Africa as a cornerstone of the British Empire. That the Boers could be persuaded to join in such a venture was largely the personal accomplishment of Campbell-Bannerman, who had termed the South African campaign barbarous; his expression of dismay and commitment to reparations had figured strongly in the Boer decision to give up the battle at the Treaty of Vereeniging in 1902. And so, after a series of conferences, the Union of South Africa was inaugurated on 31 May, 1910, at Pretoria, the Boer capital. Its first Prime Minister was not an Englishman, but a Boer, General Botha. Another Boer, a lawyer named J. C. Smuts, attained prominence during the pre-Union negotiations. He, too, was to assume the leadership of the Dominion of the British Crown in the decades to follow.

South Africa's population, by the time the Union was proclaimed, possessed all the heterogeneity it does today. The African majority had stood aloof from the Boer–British conflict, though Africans generally supported the British cause. Already confined to reserves and generally in a position of serfdom, the African population's position at the Cape and in Natal was somewhat 'better' than it was in Boer territories. The substantial 'coloured' population at the Cape had been enfranchised for a half-century, and the franchise had been extended to the Africans as well. No provision for enfranchisement existed in the Transvaal or the Orange Free State; rather, there were specific ordinances against the granting of voting rights to blacks or 'coloureds'.

What emerged at the time of Union in 1910 was not a compromise but a confirmation of the Boer doctrine. Even the timid moves towards a multiracial electorate that existed at the Cape were negated: the Union's government was to be a monopoly of white men. Campbell-Bannerman's blueprint was to restore relationships between the European settler community, and there proved to be no room for negotiations relating to the involvement of non-whites, whether African, coloured or Asian. Thus, in the half-century that the Union survived in its original form, an administration grew out of the principles for which, in essence, the Boers had fought their war. Party politics were the privilege of the white minority, and government its prerogative.

In 1919, following the end of the First World War, the Union gained control over neighbouring South West Africa, the German colony whose forces it had defeated in a brief conflict in 1915. Thus the Union, only nine years after creation, saw its sphere expanded by two-thirds of its original domain. The League of Nations' decision to award the former colonies to South Africa was not based simply on proximity, however. The South African statesman Jan Smuts was active in the development of the League's Mandate System, whereby the colonial possessions of Germany and its allies were distributed among the victorious powers. It was largely due to Smuts' efforts that South West Africa became the ward of the Union, and subsequently Smuts devoted a great deal of time towards the final incorporation of the territories into South Africa – not as a mandate, but as a fifth province.

The Second World War and the demise of the League of Nations tightened South Africa's grip on South West Africa. Although the United Nations placed the territories under its Trusteeship Council, South Africa pushed ahead with the integration of its fifth province. An attempt to deter the Union through the International Court of Justice failed, and during the 1950s and 1960s the South African presence in South West Africa became irretrievably entrenched. White residents of the territory were represented in the South African parliament and South African practices of racial-territorial separation were imposed.

In a speech before the South African Parliament during a visit in 1960, Harold Macmillan, then Prime Minister of the United Kingdom, termed Africa's drive towards self-determination and independence the 'Wind of Change'. It was a felicitous choice of words, for the process, in more ways than one, had freshness, force and direction. The initial impetus for independence was strongest in West Africa, with Ghana leading the way by becoming independent in 1957. Once this fissure in the edifice of white rule had opened up, the process assumed a greater momentum and inexorably progressed through West Africa to Equatorial and East Africa, where independence came in the early 1960s (Zaire, 1960, Tanganyika, 1961, Uganda, 1962 and Kenya, 1963). Finally, with the implosion of the moribund Portuguese empire, overt external control of African territory ended. The independent settler states of southern Africa were exposed to the full blast of the Wind of Change. White rule in the deep south, where it had assumed the pretence of an indigenous claim to legitimacy, looked so entrenched as to make the battles till then seem a mere preliminary to a final, epic struggle that might see the Europeans pushed back into the sea from whence they came.

In time the rhetoric of both sides came to promise such a total conflict. The process that led to this precipitous finale to the struggle had its origins in the somewhat contradictory route taken by the Afrikaner nation. Until 1948, and the election of a National Party government (essentially the 'Afrikaner party'), this, the majority ethnic group of the European-descended (settler) population of South Africa, had been dominated by English South African rule. The Afrikaners were descended from the early Dutch settlers – previously known as the Boers – who pioneered the European settlement of the interior in a successively futile attempt to elude British rule. By the mid-twentieth century, they had become largely sidelined into rural oblivion, a people perhaps somewhat reminiscent of the Amish in North America.

With the election of 1948, and the fast-changing postwar economic situation, the Afrikaners became, in a short space of time, a largely urbanized people. Their emergence into the commercial, industrial, urban world did not, however, lead to a more internationalist outlook. A people accustomed to extreme insularity could not make so great a leap, and their particular form of insular, religious, frontier particularism was writ large upon the face the new government presented to the outside world. The country became, in effect, one giant laager. Symbolizing South Africa's increasing isolation, not only on the African continent but also in the Commonwealth and the world, was the termination in 1961 of the Union.

Upon its election in 1948 the Nationalist Party had set in motion a process of radical change in the way South Africa was governed. The Party, representing, as it did, primarily the Afrikaner majority among the white population, instituted a programme amounting to systematic positive discrimination in favour of Afrikaners. During the period after 1948, South Africa's Nationalist government began to implement its programme of racial-territorial segregation – apartheid, the centrepiece of its aim to create a permanent Afrikaner ascendancy. This was, perhaps, the most bleakly ambitious, the most explicitly revisionist and certainly the starkest form of social engineering ever attempted, given the spatial and demographic realities of the country. In the process, the intercultural association among whites, envisaged a half-century earlier by Campbell-Bannerman and championed by Smuts and others, was rejected.

South Africa's regional thinking: post-1945 to 1970

South Africa's regional thinking after the Second World War was on a rather grand scale. Its policies invoked a deeply colonial utopia: the dream of a white republic where black neighbouring states existed only to minister to the white man's needs but otherwise discreetly and unobtrusively kept to their own place, and places, in an unalterable state of tribal innocence. In the late 1940s, General Smuts, for example, was attracted to the idea of pan-African cooperation and he urged that relations on the continent be conducted 'in the spirit of a small League of Nations'.[15]

Such a statement should be seen in the context of the time: South Africa's key relationship was with European colonial powers. This is clearly borne out in General Smuts' suggestion in 1943 of 'colonial re-organisation' in the British Empire to create new 'colonial groups' in which neighbouring Dominions would involve themselves, thus making them 'sharers and partners' in the Empire.[16] This would have given South Africa a hand in plotting Africa's future course. The Union of South Africa thus pioneered the sense of assumed superiority which concluded its dominance of the subcontinent, a mantle imbued, perhaps, by the awarding of the South West African (Namibian) mandate to the Union in 1919. The map of Africa provides a reminder of South Africa's politico-geographic good fortune when it gained Namibia. Apart from its enormous size and its not inconsiderable productive capacity, Namibia's Caprivi Strip carried the South African sphere of influence to the very banks of the Zambezi River, and to the border of Zambia.

Given its close identification with the European colonial powers, South Africa, and particularly the new government, had great difficulty in adjusting to the vastly changed postwar international environment for two reasons. First, the creation of armed independent black states raised the danger of aggression and subversion from an Africa thought highly unlikely to accept the continuance of a white racist state. Second, the weakening of western power over the continent brought the spectre of a communist advance, more or less allied to all of white South Africa's natural enemies, including colonial Indians and the Indian government, which had raised the issue of racial discrimination at the very first session of the United Nations General Assembly.[17]

The stark contrast between South African thinking and international trends in the early postwar years was nowhere more clearly illustrated than in Dr D. F. Malan's African Charter.[18] This anachronistic statement of policy in effect sought to consolidate the colonial order in Africa by, *inter alia*, declaring that the development of Africa should be guided along the line of the 'Western European Christian civilisation', and that the militarization of the 'native of Africa' should be prevented since it could endanger 'our white civilisation'.[19] As Malan enquired rhetorically at the time:

> If Africa is not preserved for Western European civilisation and if Russia obtains the ascendancy in Europe, as it may obtain it, and if the whole African continent is thrown open for communist propaganda and South Africa is the magnet for natives from the north, then I ask what the future of South Africa is going to be?[20]

South Africa's concern with creating a favourable African environment was further reflected in its participation in a series of talks on the defence of Africa and the Middle East with the colonial powers, the Commonwealth and the United States.[21] South Africa saw its defence responsibilities extending well beyond it borders and actually prepared itself (by building an armoured task force) to fight elsewhere on the continent.[22] Similarly, the sea route round the Cape and Simonstown naval base were increasingly important as the Cold War deepened. In the field of race relations, South Africa regarded it as its 'right' to give a lead to Western Europe,[23] and Prime Minister Strijdom made no secret of the fact that he considered apartheid exportable to the rest of Africa, providing the only acceptable formula for white–black relations.[24] Eric Louw, Minister for External Affairs, suggested periodic *ad hoc* discussions on common interests – of which racial policy was one – between foreign states with African interests, South Africa and Rhodesia.

While South Africa still identified with the colonial order in the 1950s, there was at the same time a growing realization that the political face of Africa was set for irrevocable change and that South Africa's fortunes no longer lay in an exclusive relationship with the colonial powers. In a celebrated statement of March 1957, Louw urged that South Africa must 'accept its future role in Africa as a vocation and must in all respects play its full part as an African power'. At the same time South Africa could become a 'permanent link between the Western nations on the one hand and the population of Africa south of the Sahara on the other'.[25] Major political developments within South Africa and in southern Africa, together with the unremitting hostility of newly independent black states towards South Africa, however, prompted it to narrow the focus from 'Africa south of the Sahara' to its immediate neighbours.

Domestic political developments were envisaged as including a complementary strand to this regional view in the form of the Bantu homeland policy as expounded by Dr H. F. Verwoerd. He envisaged that these homelands could proceed to full independence, upon which they could be linked to South Africa in a commonwealth type of relationship. The component units could be politically independent but economically interdependent.[26] They would thus form an easily controllable 'near-abroad' that formed a bridge with (or buffer against) the uncertain polities beyond. The homelands formula formed the basis of Dr Verwoerd's approach to southern Africa. At first, he wanted to draw the three High Commission Territories into the homelands and thus prevent the adoption of policies in the Territories which ran counter to separate development.[27] Although Britain refused to transfer its political guardianship of the Territories to South Africa and chose to lead them to independence according to the British recipe, Dr Verwoerd still saw a role for the Territories, when independent, in his scheme for southern African cooperation. In the political sphere, he foresaw a commonwealth evolving, which would be a consultative body of independent states 'dealing with mutual political interests'.[28] Economic links, he suggested, could be formalized in a coordinating body 'on the principles of a common market'.[29]

Reference should also be made to the place of (Southern) Rhodesia in South Africa's design for the region. South Africa and Rhodesia have experienced something of a love–hate relationship, dating back to South Africa's unsuccessful attempt to incorporate Rhodesia into the Union in the 1920s.[30] Rhodesia's Anglophilic sentiments and its membership of the Central African Federation (1953–63) prevented it from drawing closer to South Africa. However, the dissolution of the Federation paved the way for a new relationship and Dr Verwoerd was quick to suggest in 1963 that if Rhodesia was to become an independent state, it could lead to a closer relationship with the Republic, whether 'in some form of organised economic interdependence', such as in the European Economic Community, or 'for a common political interest' on the lines of the Commonwealth.[31] Ironically, the way in which Rhodesia became independent in 1965 hindered rather than helped the establishment of stronger ties, because it was politically inexpedient for South Africa to associate closely and in a formal manner with Britain's 'rebel colony'.

Vorster's great gamble

The independence of Botswana and Lesotho in 1966 and Swaziland in 1968 apparently offered South Africa the ideal opportunity to give effect to the Verwoerdian design for a commonwealth-cum-common-market arrangement in southern Africa. Verwoerd's successor, B. J. Vorster, thought in less grandiose terms – at least initially – and merely committed himself to 'maintaining the closest economic and technical co-operation among all the countries of the [southern African] region, for their mutual benefit and joint development'. He stressed that each nation thus involved would retain their political identity and therefore 'the right to choose its own political, economic and racial system'.[32] This restatement of established principles of political independence and economic interdependence was an obvious attempt to safeguard South Africa's political *status quo*. Perhaps Vorster's pragmatism was part of a grand design to move the nations slowly towards the Verwoerdian dream!

A major step towards formalizing relations was the revision, in 1969, of the Customs Union Agreement of 1909 which involved South Africa and the three former High Commission Territories (namely Basutoland, Bechuanaland and Swaziland). Another was South Africa's establishment of diplomatic relations with Malawi in 1967 – at the time, the only such links with any black state. The Portuguese territories of Angola and Mozambique drew conspicuously close to South Africa in the later 1960s. In the economic field, South Africa agreed to purchase power from the planned Ruacana Falls and Cabora Bassa hydroelectric schemes in Angola and Mozambique respectively.[33] In the military sphere, the sense of community was strengthened by the perception of a common threat in 'terrorism'.[34] Although no formal defence agreement existed, evidence suggests limited South African involvement in counter-insurgency operations in Angola and Mozambique.[35]

This successful establishment of close ties with South Africa's immediate black neighbours, together with growing domestic (white) confidence and affluence in the late 1960s, prompted the Republic to extend the frontiers of its interests in Africa.[36] In 1967 Vorster launched his so-called outward movement. It amounted to a broad-based attempt to improve South Africa's relations over a wide front,[37] but the thrust of the movement was clearly directed at Africa. Although further strengthening of ties within the southern African region was part of this outward policy, South Africa appeared more interested in bigger stakes, namely reaching a rapprochement with black states further north carrying greater political weight and which were not in any sense 'client states' of the Republic. In reality, the primary motive for wanting to play a greater part in Africa was due to the structural nature of the global economy and South Africa's declining position within it.

Despite some initial successes,[38] the dialogue initiative – as it became known – soon petered out, primarily because of the intervention of the Organization of African Unity to end moves towards rapprochement between black Africa and South Africa. This, together with South African industry's lack of global competitiveness – a point to which we shall return – led South Africa to set its sights lower and to concentrate on consolidating its position in the subcontinent and finding regional solutions to areas of conflict.

In this context, Vorster, in February 1974, defined regional cooperation in terms of a power 'bloc' of independent sovereign states. Independence was indeed a condition for membership of the bloc, in which no state would be politically or constitutionally subordinate to another and in which domestic affairs remained within the exclusive domain of each state.[39] Moves towards creating a new pattern of relations in southern Africa took a dramatic turn with Vorster's famous (or infamous) Senate speech in October 1974, in which he said 'southern Africa has come to the cross-roads', and has to choose between peace and escalating conflict. Confidently asserting that the climate for peace and normalization of relations was good, he envisaged 'peace, progress and development' in southern Africa.[40] President Kenneth Kaunda's positive response and Vorster's public commitment to reform the apartheid system in South Africa set the scene for the new era of positive regional thinking. This was the period of southern African détente, and Vorster's greatest gamble.[41]

The ruling elite within South Africa entertained high hopes for détente. Dr Muller spoke hopefully of détente drawing together the states of southern Africa in a strong bloc, which could present a common front against its common enemies.[42]

This era of détente, was however, rather short-lived. Its failures were due mainly to transformation in the international system. Among these was the oil crisis, which not only brought in its wake a prospect of oil boycotts and increased so-called third world influence on the West but also, within Africa, raised the importance of Nigeria as a rival market, for western power might betray South Africa in exchange for economic advantages in the rest of Africa. Nigeria had a definite impact on British behaviour with regard to Zimbabwe and did to some extent modify US attitudes toward Angola and Mozambique during the Carter years.

In the West's view, nothing contributed more to a sense of crisis and of doubt concerning South Africa's future than the eruption of mass struggle in the cities on an unprecedented scale, led by students and school children who had been directly influenced by the radical decolonization in southern Africa. Once more the transfer of power elsewhere raised passion and expectations in South Africa itself, now in a more militant and ideologically radical frame of reference. Economic hardship experienced by blacks as the recession began to be felt in South Africa also intensified popular resentment. It was apparent that the spirit of revolt could not long be confined to the young but would eventually engage the black working class as well, and this gave rise to an urgent search for new ways to pacify and control the urban masses. The Soweto Riots, as the urban revolt came to be known, produced a new crop of exiles who joined and, in large measure, transformed the exiled liberation movement.[43] This was to give the region new prominence in the Republic's thinking.

Reform, repression and stalemate: the era of 'total strategy'

The combined effect of all these factors was to place renewed importance on South Africa's relationship with the southern African region during the leadership of P. W. Botha. Botha faced a regional context that had changed radically. Up to the mid-1970s white rule was cushioned by the circle of settler and colonial states around it. In the

Portuguese colonies of Angola and Mozambique the metropolitan government itself, rather than settlers, had underwritten the large military effort entailed in controlling an increasingly hostile African population in the 1960s and 1970s. In 1974, when a *coup d'état* in Portugal – prompted not least by the cost of the colonial wars – displaced the fascist government, decolonization followed rapidly. Rhodesian settlers had made their unilateral declaration of independence from Britain after the break-up of the Federation in 1965, and fought their campaign against the black Zimbabwean liberation movement. But from the mid-1970s the intensity of the war became severe and despite South African assistance and an 'internal settlement', settler rule succumbed in 1979.

Zimbabwe's independence marked the final collapse of the system of white-ruled buffer states for South Africa and the final failure of its attempts to influence and contain the transfer of power on the continent. As the independence of Angola and Mozambique had done, the transfer of power to former guerrillas highlighted to white South Africans their vulnerability and the inadequacy of their previous policies for coping with decolonization in the rest of Africa and black discontent within South Africa. The Wind of Change was blowing unhindered across South Africa's frontiers, and without a radical rethink of its internal and external relations, the stark divide between black and white would likely end in the feared final bloodbath. With the balance of power and confidence radically changing in the region, there was an urgent need to create a new basis, a new structure, of domestic power and to pursue a more decisive African and international role. In effect, the sharp difference between South Africa and the rest needed to be blurred, the looming geopolitical realities diffused, and long-held certainties of the, literally, black and white situation questioned.

The South African reaction to these developments was the creation of the Constellation of Southern African States (CONSAS). The pursuit of the idea of a constellation was Botha's major foreign policy initiative and was given the same priority as his predecessor's dialogue and détente moves. Pik Botha, Minster of Foreign Affairs, even referred to it as the 'new Great Trek'.[44] The constellation idea engendered considerable support, notably among South Africa's business community and politicians. This 'establishment' enthusiasm for the notion of CONSAS must be seen against the background of South Africa and southern Africa's international position. It was clearly linked to the deterioration in the Republic's relations with the West,[45] to the escalating conflict in Namibia and Zimbabwe, to South Africa's dissatisfaction with western settlement efforts, to South Africa's failure to reach a *modus vivendi* with black states further north, and finally to threats to the Republic's own security and prosperity, particularly terrorism and sanctions. The creation of the constellation was therefore part and parcel of Botha's 'total national strategy', and featured strongly in his twelve 'policy principles'.[46]

Central to this 'total national strategy' was the hope that the 'moderate' countries of southern Africa would all share a perception that they faced a common 'Marxist threat' and could not rely on the West for support. 'It is not only the whites who stand alone at the southern point of Africa', Pik Botha argued, but 'every black leader who desired order, freedom, peace and development for his people … Also stands alone'.[47] The security of black and white was indivisible and unless they joined forces, common enemies would 'shoot us off the branch like birds, one after the other'.[48] South Africa, it would appear, not merely wished to keep Marxism out of southern Africa but intended to encourage the development of a kind of counter-ideology. After expounding the grave and evil consequences of the 'Marxist order' in his Carlton speech,[49] the Prime Minister extolled the virtues of 'a regional order within which real freedom and material welfare can be maximised and the quality of life for all can be improved'.

The promotion of this state of affairs and its resemblance to Professor J. A. Lombard's influential book entitled *Freedom, Welfare and Order*[50] was too close to be coincidental.[51] But despite the pronounced anti-Marxist strain of his exposition, P. W. Botha, in a press conference following his Carlton speech, still left open the possibility of Marxist states being included in a constellation.[52] Ideology was increasingly subordinate to the immediate need for expediency in forestalling the worst scenario of a united African front against South Africa.

The critical component of the constellation was military security. Included in Botha's vision of a 'geo-economic community of interests' was 'the concept of mutual defence against a common enemy'.[53] In the words of Pik Botha, 'countries of the sub-continent should undertake joint responsibility for the security of the region'.[54] The implications of this were clearly far reaching. Given the nature of the region, the security in question was perceived to be both external and internal; it was, moreover, often very difficult to distinguish between the two. 'Mutual defence' was taken to mean that an attack on one member was an attack on all, thus inviting a common response. It goes without saying that the 'destruction of terrorism' at the very least meant that countries would not provide sanctuary to terrorists operating against constellation partners. From the South African perspective, this would have eliminated not only the perceived threat by communist-inspired insurgents, but also more importantly the African National Congress.

The failure of this policy coincided with a new wave of international criticisms about South Africa's domestic arrangements. Power and privilege over three decades had also left their mark on the Afrikaner ruling class. Many elements of the racist ideology no longer carried conviction either as a means of understanding the complex social reality of South Africa and the world around it or, perhaps more important, as a source for strategies of 'survival'. The new strategy adopted by the Botha government was defined as a policy of winning hearts and minds at home to support total strategy against the external dangers thought to amount to a 'total onslaught' on South Africa.

The result was the subordination of all the apartheid state's policies to the defence of the national interest. Internally, the government decreed a State of Emergency, which enabled the elite to restructure the decision-making system by concentrating special powers in the office of the Prime Minister (and later of the State President). Covert operations, previously focused on espionage and political manipulation of foreign governments, were restructured to repress domestic challengers to the apartheid state.[55]

Externally, total strategy manifested itself in two forms: first, it concentrated on open or secret acts of intimidation against neighbouring states aimed at removing SWAPO and ANC forces from the borders of South Africa; second, military action, particularly the sabotage and destruction of communication systems, was designed to weaken the states of the region, to prevent them reducing their dependence on South Africa, and indeed even to increase that dependence. Significant military events were acts such as the air raids against civilian and Mozambique targets in the city of Matola in May 1983, and in 1986 the simultaneous raids against Harare, Gaborone and Lusaka, again against civilian and local targets, which deliberately coincided with, and therefore wrecked, the mission by the Commonwealth Eminent Persons Group. The blockade against Lesotho, the terrorist campaign of assassinating opponents of apartheid, even in Western European capitals, the mercenary invasion of the Seychelles – these are various examples of the intimidation strategies employed by the apartheid state to destabilize opposition to its regime, both within the region and beyond.[56]

The cost of destabilization

The cases of Mozambique and Angola give some insights into the true nature of the impact and cost of destabilization to the regional states. It is estimated that 1.5 million people died between 1980 and 1988 in these two countries alone as a direct or indirect result of destabilization. For Mozambique, destabilization shattered its economy and made it what the World Bank says is the poorest country in the world and the most indebted country in Africa.[57] This is very different from 1980 when Mozambique had a growing economy, a widely praised health service and major industrialization plans. South Africa's war, in part waged by the Renamo proxy army it supported, killed more than one million people, made five million homeless, and cost at least 11 billion pounds in damage and lost production – more than double Mozambique's total debt of £4.5 billion.

This was a war of terror – South Africa wanted to make Mozambicans afraid to use the newly built health and education system. School pupils and teachers were kidnapped. Half of all hospitals and schools were destroyed or closed. South Africa also targeted transport, commerce and export sectors. The Zambezi River Bridge is one of the longest in Africa and once carried the railway from Malawi and Mozambique's coal mines to the port of Beira. South African commandos blew up the bridge, as well as many smaller ones. South African-backed guerrillas used slave labour to destroy by hand 30 miles of railway line near Inhaminga in Mozambique. Six years after the end of the war, this railway was still closed; Mozambique had no money to repair it. By 1985, exports of sugar, tea, cashew nuts, timber and sisal were down to one-tenth of their prewar levels.

Exports of electricity, cement and coal were halted completely due to the sabotage of railway and power lines.

South Africa also imposed sanctions on Mozambique, sharply reducing use of the port of Maputo. The number of Mozambican miners who were given employment in South African mines was severely cut which significantly reduced Mozambique's earnings. Faced with this sudden loss of income, Mozambique had to buy on credit. Early debts were to Iraq, Algeria, Libya and Angola for oil. Later oil was also bought on credit from the USSR. Mozambique has always been dependent on imported consumer goods, and it had to turn to those who would sell on credit. The then socialist bloc did so, supposedly out of solidarity, but the successors to those governments – under IMF pressure – are trying to collect those debts.

Money was also borrowed for development projects that were subsequently destroyed or seriously damaged in South African attacks, including sugar mills, tea factories and a major textile mill. Railway locomotives bought on credit were destroyed. Finally, military costs escalated, and arms to defend against South African attacks were bought on credit from the Eastern bloc. As the war continued, Mozambique could not pay its debts, so they were 'rolled over' – that is, Mozambique was given new loans to pay both the capital and accumulated interest on the old loans. So it was paying interest on the interest on the interest.

Mozambique's total apartheid debt is about £4.5 billion. It is less than half of the estimate of the cost of destabilization. More than half the debt is probably accumulated interest because Mozambique is paying less than half of what is due. Of the debt, about one-third is to Russia, one-third to the industrialized countries (particularly France, Italy and Germany), and the rest divided between smaller economies such as Algeria and international agencies like the World Bank and IMF. World Bank debt is rising rapidly because Mozambique is borrowing from it to repair roads and schools destroyed by South African attacks. About £1 billion is military debt, mainly to Russia.

Mozambique is one of the first countries to go through the World Bank/IMF Heavily Indebted Poor Countries Initiative (HIPC), and this resulted in the writing off in 1999 of a substantial part of its long-term debt. Since HIPC was intended to write off only long-term debt, it has had very little impact on the actual amount the country still pays to service its external debts. During 1995–97 Mozambique paid $107 million (£64.8 million) per year in debt service; in the four years starting 1999 it will pay precisely $106 million (£64.2 million) each year. International agencies like the IMF and World Bank, as well as bilateral creditors, have agreed to write off some of Mozambique's debt, but they still insist Mozambique pay back part of the debt caused by apartheid. The country has been forced to delay the introduction of universal primary education until 2010 because of a lack of money – because money is being diverted to repay the apartheid-caused debt. In the 1980s children did not go to school because apartheid destroyed their schools and kidnapped their teachers. In the twenty-first century, Mozambican children will not go to school in order to repay money their parents and grandparents borrowed to defend themselves against apartheid.

Angola is much wealthier than Mozambique, but has been even more extensively devastated by war. The problem has been made much worse because the civil war was restarted after the results of the 1992 UN-backed election were rejected by Unita – the formerly South African and US backed guerrilla movement. More than 750 000 people died in the war to 1990; the cost is estimated at nearly £23 billion. It is estimated that another 500 000 people have died in the much more ferocious war after 1992 when there was further massive destruction. In the late 1970s and early 1980s, Angola paid for both military and development costs out of the current revenues from oil and diamonds. However, Unita and South Africa attacked export industries, notably mines and petroleum installations. Coffee and iron exports were virtually ended, and the Benguela Railway was closed. By the mid-1980s, Angola was borrowing to finance the war and the 'apartheid-caused debt' amounts to £6.4 billion. Little official information is available about Angolan debt because it has not entered into international debt renegotiations yet; at least one-third is to Russia, and a substantial part is for weapons.

While Mozambique and Angola bore the brunt of the South African assault, all the regional states were affected to some degree. South Africa imposed sanctions on Zimbabwe, disrupting its trade. It tried to cut landlocked Zimbabwe's links to the sea. Repeated attacks closed the railway line to the Mozambican port of Maputo. The oil pipeline to the Mozambican port of Beira was closed and the oil storage depot in Beira attacked by South African commandos. The railway to Beira port was repeatedly attacked and a major bridge destroyed, but Zimbabwe put substantial effort into keeping the vital railway open. It succeeded, but at one point it had 12 500 troops in Mozambique at a cost of £2 million per week. The UN's Economic Commission for Africa (ECA) estimates that extra defence spending for 1980–88 was more than £2 billion, and extra transport costs more than £400 million. Zimbabwe's apartheid-caused debt is estimated at £2.3 billion. It is a mix of military and civilian, but a substantial amount is rolled-over and rescheduled debt.

For Malawi, the main problem was that both its main links to the sea were railways through Mozambique that were cut by South African commandos and South African-backed Renamo forces. This forced all of Malawi's imports and exports to go an extra thousand miles via Zimbabwe and South Africa, which caused sharp increases in the transport costs. Many items had to be purchased in South Africa when it proved impossible to import cheaper goods. Malawi's sugar exports were halved in the 1980s, mainly due to high transport costs making exports uncompetitive. The cost to Malawi was catastrophic. As well as human suffering, Malawi had to borrow more than £700 million to pay the extra costs to feed its people. Most of Malawi's borrowing is from international financial institutions, notably the World Bank, and was intended to offset some of the costs of the blockade. Malawi also bore extra defence costs and had to support one million refugees. This continues to the present day, because the Zambezi River Bridge, and thus the rail link to Beira, remains closed, causing a permanent increase in transport costs from southern Malawi. Malawi's new democratic government is trying to redress the heritage of the 30-year Banda dictatorship and the cost of the apartheid blockade. But Malawi's creditors are insisting that it repay the apartheid-caused debt before further development loans are granted.

Zambia suffered little physical damage because of apartheid, but it paid substantial extra costs, first in 1973 when Rhodesia (then backed by apartheid South Africa) closed its border with Zambia and tried to blockade it, then when Zambia kept this border closed in order to impose UN sanctions against Rhodesia, and then in the 1970s and 1980s when its rail links through Angola and Mozambique were cut. This isolation was a major reason for the construction of the Tazara railway to Dar es Salaam. As well as higher transport costs, it can be argued that the isolation of Zambia made it more difficult for it to diversify from its dependence on copper. Zambia also paid substantially increased defence costs in this period.

Zambia's apartheid-caused debt is £1.9 billion. Half of Zambia's debt is to the IMF, World Bank and African Development Bank; the other half is bilateral. Many of the loans were given as 'aid' in the face of both destabilization and lower prices for copper, Zambia's main export; some (including early SADCC loans) relate to the Tazara railway and the oil pipeline to Dar es Salaam, which were constructed to avoid South Africa. Destabilization costs are estimated at £3.8 billion. Botswana, Lesotho and Swaziland were significantly less seriously affected by South Africa, in part because they were small and were members of a customs union with South Africa. They did, however, take strong stands against apartheid, and were punished by various blockades and bloody raids. This pushed up transport and defence costs. Three-quarters of Lesotho's debt is with the international financial agencies, and a significant amount relates to the Highland Water Scheme – largely forced on Lesotho by apartheid South Africa (Table 1.1).

Conclusion

In addition to the monetary costs of destabilization noted in this chapter, the climate of conflict and hostility under the policy also

Table 1.1   Apartheid debt

Country	Apartheid debt in billions of dollars	Debt payments as % of total trade earnings
Angola	6 432	17
Botswana	152	5
Lesotho	91	6
Malawi	724	21
Mozambique	4 545	42
Swaziland	0	3
Tanzania	492	23
Zambia	1 905	25
Zimbabwe	2 273	24
Subtotal	16 614	
South Africa	11 345	12
Total	27 959	

had a number of less documented but equally devastating impacts on the region. In terms of human security, large numbers of people were displaced by the apartheid-sponsored wars in Angola and Mozambique. According to recent statistics, there were over a million Mozambique refugees in other SADC countries at the beginning of the 1990s, while a further 200 000 to 300 000 had secured some limited protection in the South African 'homelands' of kaNgwane and Gazankulu. Similarly 300 000 Angolans had sought refuge in Zaire, 100 000 in Zambia and 40 000 in Namibia in the period before the signing of the 1991 Bicesse ceasefire accord. Military expenditure also rose appreciably across the region and in the most extreme cases – Angola and Mozambique – came to account for over 40 per cent of total state expenditure by the end of the 1980s. The result was to put greater pressure on already scarce resources and to marginalize the people of the region further.

Destabilization, however, eventually produced its contradictions. By the end of the 1980s any potential benefits created for South African exporters by undercutting efforts to diversify was more than offset by the negative impact on the capacity of regional states to import. At the same time, South Africa's growing need for physical inputs – water and electricity – from the rest of the region became increasingly apparent. A growing recognition on the part of South Africa's business community that some form of restabilization of the regional economy was in South Africa's own interest can be identified as an important factor leading to the turn away from destabilization policies by the state in the late 1980s.

2
South Africa: from Apartheid to Democracy

There the victims parade with no mask to hide the brutish reality – the beggars, the prostitutes, the street children, those who seek solace in substance abuse, those who have to steal to assuage hunger, those who have to lose their sanity because to be sane is to invite pain . . . Among us prowl the products of our immoral and amoral past.

Deputy President Thabo Mbeki, 8 May 1996

Apartheid was derivative of the type of 'native' policies which saw colonial populations as needing managing in a way that recognized their position outside 'mainstream, modern' society, while retaining the availability of their labour. Yet it needed to be something more than previous policies to achieve the Nationalist goal of creating a permanent Afrikaner ascendancy that was based on control of a burgeoning modern, industrial economy. The rigid racial demarcations of Afrikaner-controlled rural society needed to be preserved in the growing cities, in opposition to the habitual characteristic of cities as cultural, and increasingly racial, melting pots. In this context, apartheid's principle historical mission was not to force a rupture with the past but to smooth the transition to a changed political economy after the Second World War for all categories of white people, subject, to be sure, to Afrikaner political dominance. Economically it was a means of facilitating the development of an Afrikaner bourgeoisie that would also bring material improvement to all classes of Afrikaners.[1] But it was much more than this: it facilitated the transition from an economy based on mining and agriculture, heavily dependent on a colonial labour regime, to one increasingly reliant on manufacturing that could, in theory at least, do without the full panoply of labour repression.[2]

Apartheid arbitrated between the competing demands of industrial employers of the new type and the older sectors of the economy for cheap black labour. In doing so it prevented any gains in industrial and political power that changing economic structures might bring, thereby guaranteeing the suppression of black wages in order to sustain high wages for whites across the whole economy.[3] It was able to create increased employment opportunities for Afrikaners in an expanding state sector, and through state expansion to sustain a high level of expenditure that had the desired Keynesian effect on economic growth.[4] In short, Afrikaner nationalism secured the incorporation of Afrikaners into metropolitan capitalism, which they had previously denounced as imperialist, and reconciled them to it. In this way, it was able to guarantee political and industrial tranquillity in a time of transformation, at the expense, needless to say, of blacks. The racist strategy for development incorporated the repressive elements of colonial production into the postcolonial political economy, while at the political and cultural level it perpetuated colonialism. This unique position helped to create a happy marriage between global capital and domestic capitalism for over fifty years. So why did it suddenly collapse in the late 1980s? And what has replaced it? These are the two questions at the heart of this chapter.

Apartheid

Like Fascism, Nazism and Communism, Apartheid as an ideology was based on a particular understanding of history and a perception of how the future should be constructed. The theorists of apartheid drew upon a legacy of cultural nationalists who believed in a God-given mission of the Afrikaner people. The Afrikaans language, the Calvinist theology of the Dutch Reformed Church and the tales of the Great Trek bestowed a sentiment of unique identity whose destiny apartheid was meant to protect. The theory called for the separate development in accordance with inherent characteristics of South Africa's diverse people. In the words of its apologists, separateness expressed 'the desire of the Afrikaner people to find a lasting and ethically just solution to the Union's colour problem in general, and the native question in particular.' In practice, separate development rationalized a project of racial domination and material privilege.

As mentioned, the apartheid system built upon existing Native Policy, but as a function of its mechanistic logic, greatly strengthened and standardized existing policies of inequality. In the colonial era native policy had come about mainly through expediency rather than grand design. This is evidenced by colonial populations even within one part of one Empire – the British Union of South Africa – being subject to plural varieties of governance: from the partially enfranchised of the Cape to the very indirectly ruled feudal subjects of the proxy kingdoms of the highlands. Apartheid took this system a large step further; it was the archetypal grand design, concluding that development paths of the 'races' were divergent and therefore irreconcilable. The only solution was for each to follow its own path, at its own pace, thereby not imposing upon the others.

Putting apartheid into practice meant a standardization of the criteria of racial type. Local differences of political representation of the various populations needed to be eliminated and rigid demarcations established. Economic, religious, spatial and gender considerations were all subordinate to the 'racial'. Each race was expected to play out the role attributed to it. Needless to say this led to considerable shoehorning of various groups into their perceived roles. Consider the position of urban blacks, for example. Blacks were expected to have a tribal affinity. The cosmopolitan blacks who comprised much of the urban population had often long lost any such tribal affinity in the space of several generations of urban living. They were joined by many others who flooded in during the war, eager to escape rural constraints. All were to be assigned tribal identities, often spuriously so, as a preliminary to the establishment of the homelands policy. Needless to say practically all these hardships fell upon the majority black population, but the relatively privileged 'coloureds', and 'Indians' were also subject to eviction and unfavourable zoning.

Many of these basic aspects of apartheid had no great immediate impact on the rural black population whose lives had always been a litany of toil and abuse, but for those in urban areas they represented a massive dashing of expectations. To understand this it is worth looking at the parallel urbanization of American blacks, from a similar rural, segregated life. The great migration from the south to the northern industrial belt led to great improvements in lifestyle for many, on the back of the American consumer boom. While great relative differences of income still existed, there were still considerable absolute gains. The vast bulk of the South African population was denied an equivalent improvement – most were increasingly worse off. Whether this positive immiseration was a conscious decision of apartheid planning is not entirely clear, but keeping the black population poor led to one of the great long-term contradictions of apartheid that its founders failed to foresee.

The philosophical underpinnings of the system were premised on a notion of superiority, but unlike other such ideologies, this was a superiority complex based as much on fear – fear of the numeric superiority of the African. Unlike the indigenous peoples overrun by other settler societies – the Americans, Australians and New Zealanders – the African in southern Africa was far more resilient, less affected by pandemic disease and proving a real military threat for a longer period. The Boers had always felt greatly outnumbered in the land they claimed, and this fear was codified in the strong spatial element of apartheid policy – the need to keep the distance within. Urban areas of all sizes throughout South Africa had always had quite a strong element of segregation. Apartheid took this to a literal extreme with the introduction of separate staircases, park benches, etc.

The introduction of apartheid more or less coincided with the high point of European numbers relative to African. Once ensconced in their suburbs, like other industrial societies, the white South Africans forsook large families for the swimming pool and the new BMW. The black South African faced with no such choice, doomed to perpetual poverty, failed to pass through 'demographic transition'. Cheap black labour as an out-and-out asset to the white economy gave way to concern over increasingly large structural unemployment, evidenced by the huge, sprawling townships outside the major cities. The teeming masses of the townships threatened the possibility of maintaining a viable distance between black and white, with the result that the instigation of the homeland policy took on a new importance to the regime.

The idea of a fast-growing and increasingly hostile black population must have registered with the Afrikaner elite in the final decades of apartheid. The fate of the Rhodesians and the Portuguese settlers showed the inevitable consequences of a protracted guerrilla war. Such a war had not been possible for the resistance to carry off as yet because of the iron grip the security services could still exercise over much of the country. In the Rhodesian and Portuguese wars, the native populations in vast tracts of the country were virtually cut off from the writ of the government in any meaningful sense. The guerrilla armies had had the possibility of moving through a 'sea' of people who could sustain and hide them. In many areas the government only showed its face through occasional patrols or overflying aircraft. The Rhodesians, learning from the British Malayan experience, attempted to address this problem with the formation of local militias, under Sithole and Muzorewa, but it was too little, too late.

The South Africans were aided by the regional geography. Even if Botswana and Namibia had been able to allow guerrilla bases on their territory from which to launch attacks, they would have had to cross many miles of open scrub and semi-desert terrain. The only viable incursion possibilities were across the Limpopo from Zimbabwe and Mozambique. The former's infrastructure was too vulnerable to RSA attack to allow overt guerrilla operations. The Mozambique border was sufficiently short for the RSA security forces to cover it fairly effectively. Entering South Africa would still leave guerrilla groups vulnerable. Apart from parts of the 'homelands', the countryside was hostile, controlled by white farmers to an extent that large areas of the former colonies never were. In this sense the Afrikaners' spatial proximity to the black population served them well. The only recourse open to the resistance was a terrorist campaign, and this was notably successful on occasions. This had the effect of wrong-footing the Afrikaners. They were certainly prepared for an insurgency conflict, and had perhaps the most effective counter-insurgency force ever seen. Urban terrorism emanating from the increasingly impenetrable townships posed an unknown threat. Both in practical and psychological terms the whites felt vulnerable in a way that they had not expected. The South African economy had a far more complex infrastructure than the other white-ruled states. An ongoing terrorist campaign would have been enormously expensive and greatly detrimental to urban-white, civilian morale.

The liberation struggle

An examination of the cognitive factors affecting the collapse of the apartheid regime highlights four principal areas of interest: the role of the black consciousness movement, the ANC and UDF, the trade unions and the international community.

The role of black consciousness

In retrospect, it is clear that black consciousness was more of an intellectual orientation than a political grouping, difficult to capture analytically because it was represented by a scattering of proponents and small organizations rather than a single party. Protagonists asserted a confidence in being black in the wake of bannings, everyday racism and dehumanization. They took on the apartheid state precisely at the time when its economic success was cresting, and the relentless propaganda in favour of apartheid and retribalization was gaining ground.

The use of the word 'black' was in itself a dialectical challenge to apartheid's ethnic and racial terminology and an alternative to the negative 'non-white' (*nie blanke*) or 'non European' which was in common currency. Terminology has been a critical part of both the construction and projection of apartheid as the government's adoption of the word 'Bantu' rather than native or African testifies. As in the United States, where the African-American shifted from 'Negro' and 'coloured' to black, the use of the word in South Africa was equally a monumental shift in the native struggle against apartheid. Black specifically included people of mixed origin – the so-called 'coloured' and Indian people – as well as Africans.

The amalgam of ideas that made up black consciousness drew on the heritage of pan-Africanism as well as the populist language of the US civil rights and Black Power movements in the late 1960s. It articulated a form of self-expressive identity which was autonomous of the ruling cultural, educational and government systems, an attempt to define blackness in its own terms, from its own starting point rather than as an opposition or counter to white culture. This creation of a self-confident, politicized movement working from its own frame of reference allowed blacks to cope with the psychological aspect of the struggle far more effectively.

The black consciousness movement (which had its heyday in the late 1960s), was in many ways the spark which ignited the tinder of African revolt. It is noteworthy that the interesting thing about the black consciousness movement was that it was oriented to the critical reconstruction of the 'consciousness' of the diverse components of the African majority, its goal being very much the re-externalization of the internalized racial ascription as a means of forging a socially powerful inclusive concept of critical black unity. Indeed, as the Vaal uprising of 1984 illustrates, what was interesting about the 1980s black consciousness movement was the linkages people made between local grievances and national political and economic changes. No longer prepared to tolerate rent hikes, exploitative labour conditions, appalling living conditions, inadequate education and corrupt, state-appointed local councillors, the Vaal residents directed their anger at anything representative of apartheid capitalism.

It was partly the implicit anti-capitalist content of the Vaal uprising, and the subsequent nationwide mass struggle, that gave the black consciousness movement a historic opportunity for realizing a radically transformative politics in the 1980s. In this sense black consciousness addressed the diatribe of the state on its own terms, and threw it back at them.

The role of the ANC and United Democratic Front

As Alfred Nzo, the then secretary-general of the ANC, rightly noted, 'the primary objective of the liberation struggle was not aimed at reforming apartheid, but rather to bring about the radical political, economic, social and cultural transformation of South Africa.' Although by the 1970s most of the organization's leaders had either been imprisoned or murdered by the ruthless security police, the remnants fled abroad establishing offices in London, Lusaka and other capitals from which they mounted campaigns which secured the sports boycott, the 1977 arms embargo and the exclusion of South Africa from the United Nations and other international organizations.

The radicalization of the ANC was evident in the rising incidence and boldness of acts of sabotage, including the bombing at the Keoberg nuclear power station in 1982 and the 1983 Pretoria bombing. Within the anti-apartheid movement inside South Africa, these acts of defiance against the Pretoria regime enhanced the ANC's popularity. It is estimated that nearly 7000 new recruits left South Africa and joined the ANC in exile between 1980 and 1983. It was largely this context of the neighbouring states helping the ANC against the Pretoria regime that influenced the creation of CONSAS. As was noted earlier, and in spite of the official rhetoric, the idea behind CONSAS was to extend Pretoria's opposition to subversive activities to the region. In other words, CONSAS would have legitimated the replication of the brutal domestic tactics against the opponents of the regime to the neighbouring states. But an alternative organization linking the black governments of the region, the Southern African Development Coordination Conference (SADCC), though beset by problems, confirmed the frontline states' commitment to finding a political and economic future outside South Africa's orbit.

It was the failure of this approach to deal with the armed wing of the ANC, together with the feeling of isolation as a result of the collapse of Rhodesia, that invoked the South African policy of destabilization of the region. In rereading this 'dark period' of apartheid history, it is clear that the ANC problematized the idea of a white South African nationhood as it argued for the idea of 'the people' and 'the nation' which would not be racially exclusive, but which would instead allow for a multiracial franchise, and hence for the extension of citizenship rights (including the rights to membership of the South African nation) to all the inhabitants of the territory of South Africa. The ANC's commitment to a radical reconstruction of the state in accordance with non-racial liberal values can be witnessed in the ANC's continued commitment to the principles outlined in the Freedom Charter (1955).[5] It therefore emphasized the invalidity and illegitimacy of the structure of the homelands and the marginalization of the African in urban areas in the townships. In the quest for racial inclusivity, '[it] eschewed absolute ideological coherence in favour of the most inclusive possible unity, to be forged into a non-racial South African nation dedicated to isolating and confronting minority domination'.[6]

The politicization of the trade union movements

From the 1960s to the early 1970s, the apartheid state was quite successful in restricting the activities of the urban and migrant workers in the political sphere. This was done through imposing strict working regimes and laws on the labour force. These laws were designed to restrict labour demands to economic matters. In general, politically active trade union leaders were often detained without trial, subjected to torture, charged with treason and so forth. In the 1980s this strategy of intimidation and coercion failed to prevent a split from occurring within the trade union movement over the issue of whether they should become directly involved in the liberation struggle.

This issue was resolved in the unity conference which resulted in the formation of Congress of South African Trade Unions (COSATU) in December 1985, and the dissolution into it of the Federation of South African Trade Unions, which had been, at least at leadership level, the major protagonist of the restricted role of the trade unions. Although the black trade union movement was still not fully united, and divisions between COSATU on the one side and CUSA and AZACTU still existed, albeit on a diminishing scale, nevertheless the formation of COSATU in December 1985 united a large number of unions in a federation on the basis of a commitment to the broad aims of the national liberation movement. In the same years, a delegation under Cyril Ramaphosa (the then general secretary of the National Union of Mineworkers) met the ANC in Lusaka to negotiate their role in the liberation struggle. This was to mark the official period of trade union politicization in the liberation struggle against the apartheid government.

Where black consciousness critically challenged the state's racial aspirations among the African community and the ANC (UDF) took issue with the state's explicit affirmation of a racially exclusive white nation, the trade union movement problematized the idea of the state as an interest-free political association which did not play beggar to economically powerful classes. They identified the notion that the apartheid state could in no way be understood if it was abstracted from the power asymmetries and class conflict imminent within civil society. By rejecting the idea of the economic neutralism of the state and acknowledging the intimate connection between a developing apartheid state and particular private capital (i.e. white) they shattered the idea of the state as a political association which could provide for the prosperity of its subjects on equal terms.

International sanctions

The gradual implementation of sanctions was an expression of the growing abhorrence at the regime and at its dogmatic refusal to give any ground in a fast changing world. This sentiment on the part of the international community was gradually changed into practical action, which generally, though not universally, took the form of sanctions and financial disinvestment in South Africa.[7] These sanctions were, in many ways, a response both to African attempts to publicize their experience of oppression and to their rejection of the idea of the legitimacy of the apartheid state on a national and international level, and also to the state's non-compensatory attitude towards the African majority.[8]

Beginning in the 1950s, the ANC had appealed to the international community to implement boycotts against South African products in order to register its moral opposition to apartheid. This was soon expanded to calls for the United Nations General Assembly to implement comprehensive and mandatory trade and arms boycotts on the apartheid state. However, it was not until 1977 that the UN Security Council imposed a mandatory arms boycott, and only in 1985 that the Council urged the General Assembly to impose comprehensive trade sanctions.

The success of sanctions has only belatedly come to be recognized. In assessing their impact on South Africa, however, we need to acknowledge that the options available to the international community were quite limited in both scope and impact. This was partly the result of vested interests, but mostly it was because of South Africa's economic position. On the basis of purely national data, it has long been asserted that South Africa's rate of growth was among the highest in the world throughout the post-1945 period. The single most important sector was manufacturing. The economy had grown rapidly from 1950 onwards through industrialization, with manufacturing accounting for over 23 per cent of GDP in 1980, compared with 14 per cent in 1946. Indeed, as a whole, the share of the primary sector in GDP declined from 31.7 per cent in 1950 to 18.4 per cent in 1984, while the share of the secondary sector rose from 14.1 per cent to 25.5 per cent over the same period.[9] In 1990, the share of agriculture as a percentage of GDP was just 5 per cent, while manufacturing rose to 26 per cent (see Table 2.1). As is evident from Table 2.1, with the exception of South Africa and Zimbabwe, manufacturing contributes less than 15 per cent of GDP for most of the southern African countries. Furthermore, as cited in the 1987 SADC annual report, manufacturing activities involve mostly agricultural products.[10] Nearly all of their exports are in the form of primary products. In 1992, for instance, the Southern African Development Community (SADC) countries' total exports and imports (excluding South Africa and Mauritius) were estimated at US$103 billion and US$115 billion respectively, with mineral exports accounting for about 60 per cent and the remaining 40 per cent being made up of mostly agricultural commodities such as coffee, sugar, tea, tobacco, etc.[11] Combined manufacturing exports in the SADC countries represent less than 20 per cent of regional exports, and less than 10 per cent if South Africa is excluded (see Table 2.1).

In view of the dire state of the regional manufacturing sector, South Africa was able to produce a range of products which – while not being competitive on the international markets – were nonetheless very competitive regionally. Thus, although the production of manufactured goods was largely oriented to the domestic market, South Africa found itself in a position where it had near total monopoly over the regional economies. Since then, export of manufactured goods to the region has contributed significantly to South Africa's economic growth. A study conducted in the 1970s, for example, found that although the combined GDP of Botswana, Lesotho and Swaziland was at the time only 3 per cent that of South Africa, trade with these countries was responsible for 27 per cent of new value added and around 67 000 new jobs in South Africa's manufacturing sector.[12]

No comparable study for later years or a broader range of trading partners is known to exist, but available statistics point to a continuing disproportionate importance of regional and sub-Saharan trade

Table 2.1   Structure of production as a percentage of GDP, 1990

Country	Agriculture	Manufacturing[1]	Other industrial sectors	Service sector
Angola	13	4	40	43
Botswana	3	6	51	40
Lesotho[2]	24	14	16	46
Malawi	33	14	6	46
Mozambique	65	–	15	21
Namibia	11	5	33	50
Tanzania	59	10	2	29
Zambia[2]	17	43	12	29
Zimbabwe	13	26	14	47
South Africa	5	26	18	51

Notes: 1. Comprises value added in mining, manufacturing, construction, electricity, water and gas.
   2. Figures relating to manufacturing in Lesotho and Zambia seem inflated.
Source: ADB, *Economic Integration in Southern Africa*, Vol. 1, 1993, 377.

Table 2.2   SADC manufacturing exports – 1988, (US$ m)

Country	Total exports	Manufacturing exports	Manufactured as % of total
Angola	2 466	11	0.5
Botswana	1 479	38	2.6
Lesotho	54	16	19.6
Malawi	103	8	7.8
Mauritius	–	–	–
Namibia	947	44	4.7
Swaziland	469	58	12.4
Tanzania	402	73	18.2
Zambia	1 179	25	2.1
Zimbabwe	1 592	284	17.8
South Africa	21 549	4583	21.2
SADC total	30 532	5190	17.0

Source: Compiled from statistics from various sources.

for manufactured exports. Figures for 1985, the last year when trade statistics were fully published in South Africa, shows that while trade with non-Southern African Customs Union (SACU) African countries was responsible for only 4 per cent of total SACU exports, this trade accounted for 36 per cent of exports of machinery, 28 per cent of chemical products, 27 per cent of vehicles and transport equipment, 14 per cent of miscellaneous manufactured goods, 10 per cent of processed foods and a considerable percentage of the total export of other less important manufactured consumer goods (see Table 2.3).[13] As Table 2.3 indicates, the region has formed the only assured and successful market for many industrial goods; approximately 10 per cent of South Africa's were of manufacturing origin by the late 1980s.[14] Many of these figures (see Table 2.3) would, moreover, undoubtedly have been much higher had they referred to South African trade with all African countries (including other SACU members). This is particularly the case for many of the more capital intensive and technologically advanced sectors (e.g. machinery, chemicals, vehicles, etc.).

More recent figures confirm the continued importance of regional and sub-Saharan markets for South Africa's manufacturing sector (see Table 2.3). Thus while total trade with non-SACU African countries made up less than 10 per cent of the total exports in 1990,

Table 2.3   Trade of SACU members with other African countries, 1985 (rand million)

Section of CCN nomenclature	Export	Import	Total export of the section	South Africa's % of total export of the section
Live animals/animal products	43.5	7.7	331.0	13
Vegetable products	78.9	38.5	868.9	9
Animal and vegetable fats	17.2	5.7	76.1	23
Prepared foodstuffs, beverages	79.7	91.7	808.3	10
Mineral products	288.4	21.0	4 996.0	6
Chemical products	262.1	9.5	930.7	28
Artificial resins, plastics	71.2	2.5	153.8	46
Skins, leather products	1.5	9.3	272.0	1
Wood products	13.8	20.1	106.5	13
Paper products	50.5	4.9	657.0	8
Textiles	51.8	83.6	1 044.8	5
Footwear	5.6	4.4	12.3	46
Stoneware	27.2	1.2	85.3	32
Precious metals, stones	1.4	52.3	2 607.1	0
Base metals	267.0	53.4	4 045.9	7
Machinery	189.3	20.0	529.6	36
Transport equipment	96.0	8.0	361.3	27
Optical and medical equipment	13.6	3.4	74.5	18
Miscellaneous	6.2	4.1	44.2	14
Works of art	0.0	0.7	23.0	0
Other unclassified	13.8	14.8	18 747.4	0
Total	1579.0	457.0	36 775.8	4
(Total 1984)	(891.7)	(485.2)	(25 585.9)	(4)

Note: Totals may not add up precisely, due to rounding of section figures.
Source: Republic of South Africa, *Foreign Trade Statistics, Calendar Year 1985* (Pretoria: Government Printer).

this trade accounted for no less than 32 per cent of South Africa's manufacturing exports. The upswing in this trade since the end of the 1980s is reported to have given an important boost to South Africa's steel, food, chemical and motor vehicle industries among others.[15] Commentators have also suggested that increasing sales to African countries made a major contribution to the sharp rise in export of such 'non-traditional' items as 'plastic and rubber products' or 'miscellaneous manufactured goods', which rose by 42 per cent and 41 per cent respectively between 1990 and 1991.[16]

As a result, South Africa's economic advantage in the region – and for that matter, on the continent – is quite considerable. With the exceptions of Angola and Tanzania, South African capital has been the primary source of investment for the rest of the SADC members. In Zimbabwe, for example, an estimated 25–30 per cent of privately owned capital stock is estimated to be South African, although there has been a small reduction since 1985. It is estimated that South Africans own approximately 40 per cent of registered industrial enterprises in Botswana. In Zambia, South Africa owns key mining and engineering firms and dominates the freight and forwarding business throughout the region.[17]

It was largely this dominance and South Africa's continental role that made sanctions very difficult to implement. When they were implemented, they did not restrict imports of strategic minerals; nor did they, in themselves, seriously affect financial links or transfers of technology. They were thus full of loopholes. Nevertheless, as the Commonwealth Expert Study Group on sanctions concluded, 'partial sanctions produced partial success'.[18] Historically, and in almost all environments, sanctions have been most effective when targeted at a country's exports rather than its imports. Thus, aside from the military embargo, South Africa experienced few difficulties in obtaining technology.[19] Indeed, the short-term consequences of the disinvestment campaign may even have had a positive effect, transferring ownership to South African enterprises. Transnational corporations (TNCs) responded to divestment pressures by using a variety of non-equity channels to transfer technology. However, sanctions directed at South Africa's exports were remarkably effective. Nine key countries alone (the USA, Denmark, Canada, Finland, Norway, Sweden, France, Australia and New Zealand) reduced their imports from South Africa between 1983 and 1987 by $1.25 billion, a reduction equivalent to 12 per cent of South Africa's non-gold exports and 7 per cent of total exports.[20]

Most clearly, it is apparent that the financial sanctions imposed during the mid-1980s played a major role in preparing the ground for the political liberation which emerged in white politics during and after the 1989 election. This was a result of a strategic convergence (albeit not a planned one) between the ANC-led international anti-apartheid forces and western governments, banks and international financial institutions during the last quarter of the 1980s. As the following passage from the sanctions report commissioned by the Australian government clearly illustrates, this was truly an alliance of convenience:

> It is one of the ironies of the peace process in southern Africa that it owes its existence, at least in part, to the actions of western bankers ... What the financial sanctions have done is to reinforce tendencies that were already present in apartheid itself ... the financial sanctions work with and not against tendencies inherent in the economy of international finance. South Africa is being excluded from the world stock of savings not because bankers and financiers are ideologically united in their detestation of apartheid ... but because most of them now see South Africa as a bad risk. [T]he financial sanctions are almost ideal, because ... it is by and large a sanction that market forces work to encourage.[21]

So the often understated role of sanctions had more resonance than, perhaps, they are usually given credit for. Even so, *ceteris paribus*, regimes have survived far worse economic stricture than that endured by the white South African. It is easy to overstate the inevitability of the effect of sanctions. A hypothetical scenario whereby apartheid survived through to the present day might see it finding a whole range of pariah, or maverick, states with which to trade. The increasingly arcane nature of global financial movements might also have served to allow an avenue for capitalization of the Republic's economy.

The collapse of apartheid

The decisive blow for the apartheid system came when early in 1989 the then president of the National Party, P. W. Botha, was incapacitated by a stroke. After continuing for several months to cling onto the last vestiges of his terrifying power, some less than honourable swordsmanship by F. W. de Klerk behind the scenes forced him to abdicate, and before the end of the year de Klerk was himself in power. Deep down there was little difference between the mad old king and the new leader of the pack, and de Klerk's history in politics prior to 1989 is a disquieting display of rightist moves and expedient, self-serving manoeuvres.[22] Indeed, what was notable about his political style was his rigid loyalty to the National Party and all that it stood for. He conformed faithfully to every party policy of the time, whether it was under the mantle of Strydom or Verwoerd or Vorster, or subsequently P. W. Botha. Over the years he had spoken out adamantly against integrated sport, mixed marriages, trade union rights for blacks and black claims for permanent residence in white South Africa. Above all he was a forceful proponent of the National Party's policy on racial groupings, of keeping apart, by law wherever necessary, South Africa's four racial groups – blacks, whites, coloureds and Indians.

When in power, however, De Klerk had one faculty his predecessors lacked: he was not a slave to ideology, and was endowed with a canny instinct for political survival. He had no illusion about the situation into which history, with more than a little nudge from himself, had thrust him. Since 1985, South Africa had been governed under successive states of emergency to enable the government to deal with internal revolt against apartheid. Black political organizations had been banned, thousands of dissidents had been detained, the army and paramilitary police had been used to crush township 'unrest' and strict censorship had been imposed on the media. Abroad South Africa was treated as a pariah state, shunned in international political circles and subjected to trade sanctions and sports boycotts. Foreign bankers had inflicted their own sanctions by refusing to provide new loans, and scores of foreign corporations had decided to withdraw from the country.

Although authoritarian by nature and intolerant of opposition, what shook de Klerk's confidence in the merits of white rule was the mounting cost of apartheid. As was noted in earlier chapters, Botha's legacy was a country not only bereft of a viable political system but also afflicted by deep economic malaise. Faced with this legacy, de Klerk was forced to steer a middle course between the complete dismantling of the increasingly costly and unsustainable apartheid system and the rigid opposition of white nationalists to any changes at all. Initially de Klerk sought to appeal to white and black 'moderates' at home and abroad who would accept reform as a substitute for a transition to a black-run government dominated by the ANC. He was confident that the plan he had in mind for 'power sharing' among different racial groups would find sufficient allies to make it a viable proposition. All would depend on negotiation. The government meanwhile would remain firmly in control until it was satisfied that the deal had been struck.

Negotiating the transition necessitated the release of Nelson Mandela and the unbanning of the ANC in 1990. It also ended emergency rule in most provinces by the end of the year. Through much of 1991 the opposing sides could not get beyond talks about how to start negotiating. Later that year, rising violence, looming economic disaster and the dead-end into which apartheid had forced South Africa internationally induced de Klerk to confront the white electorate about the future of the apartheid state.[23] This was the background to the March referendum in 1992. During the campaign, reformers warned of an economic catastrophe if the referendum were rejected; the ANC, though angered by another white-only vote, also urged a 'yes' vote to avoid civil war. The gamble paid off: de Klerk was endorsed by 68.7 per cent of South Africa's 15 per cent voting electorate. Despite great tensions, especially after the killing of Chris Hani the secretary-general of the Communist Party by a right-wing extremist, the government and the ANC drew closer. Late in 1993, after much compromise on all sides, an interim constitution was unveiled, which was subsequently implemented with a full and democratic election in April 1994. Against all expectations, the elections were peaceful. The ANC won 62 per cent of the overall votes. The National Party trailed with 20 per cent and the Inkatha Freedom Party surprisingly got nearly 10 per cent. The other parties did poorly, but the nature of the electoral system ensured some seats for most of them in the new parliament.

South Africa's challenges

After the country's first multi-party elections in 1994 the new democratic government unveiled a package of reforms collectively called the Reconstruction and Development Programme (RDP). This was the grand blueprint to transform South African society through reforming and redefining the patterns of ownership, influence and power. The total cost of the plan was estimated at R100 billion (£20 billion) over five years. Its priorities included the meeting of basic needs, developing human resources, building the economy, democratizing the state, improving welfare and housing and educating the large illiterate sections of its society. The overall goal of the RDP was 'to reinvent South Africa and create a brave new non-racial [country]'.[24] The RDP ran into trouble almost straight away. Its implementation was scheduled to take place through a special RDP fund, financed fundamentally by reallocation expenditure from the regular government departments. For 1994–95, 2.5 billion rand were budgeted, to be increased gradually to 12.5 billion in 1998–99. However, due to a lack of spending capacity, especially at the local level where the administrative machinery was not yet in place, 1.7 billion rand had to be carried forward to 1995–96 and it was calculated that at least 20 per cent of the RDP budget for the following fiscal year would be spent in 1996–97, at the earliest.

Five years on, it is very difficult to see the immediate impact of this policy. Indeed, it is hard to avoid the conclusion that for the vast majority of indigenous South Africans, the formal removal of political apartheid has done very little to eliminate their poverty. It appears that the removal of political apartheid has been replaced by economic apartheid. The only difference is that economic apartheid has been legitimated by two-thirds of South Africa's voting electorate. The central policy of the new government's domestic strategy, Growth, Employment and Redistribution (GEAR), for instance, provides a poignant example of this trend. Although this policy has been presented in a high-profile manner, jobs continue to be shed by the tens of thousands, and substantive redistribution to the general population remains illusionary. The ANC leadership has changed from a revolutionary activist group to the very model of a modern capitalist elite, boasting of their low balance of payment deficit and devoted to monetarist economics. The governor of the South African Reserve Bank, Chris Stahls, has even criticized the 'inflexible' working practices of a people who barely earn a living wage, while allowing many of South Africa's huge corporations to transfer billions of South African rands to their offshore subsidiaries. Finance Minister Trevor Manuel's deficit-reducing 1999 budget ahead of the June general elections drew praise from the finance professionals, who congratulated him for 'balancing the books'. Manuel also announced a cut in the corporate tax rate from 35 per cent to 30 per cent, which was calculated to appeal to foreign investors. He also estimated a GDP growth of around 1.8 per cent by the end of the year rising to 3.8 per cent in 2000. Unfortunately these rates will not do the trick. Even if the South African economy were to soar to 8.5 per cent growth – an impossible dream – it would take ten years to provide employment for all those out of a job.

The challenges facing the new democratic government are numerous. The economy is growing too slowly to provide jobs for the overwhelming numbers of unemployed people, and the hopeless jobless add to the crisis of crime, violence and AIDS. This list is by no means exhaustive: migration, poverty, homelessness and illiteracy can all be added to the national agenda that awaits the fledgling democracy as it heads into the new millennium.

The economy

South Africa is the giant not just of southern Africa but of sub-Saharan Africa, accounting for 45 per cent of the continent's gross national product (GNP). In comparative terms, this figure is 50 per cent greater than that of its nearest rival, Algeria, and two and half times more than that of Nigeria and Egypt. Although it has only one-third of the population of the subcontinent, South Africa has three-quarters of the region's GNP and its per capita GNP is almost two-and-a-half times that of the regional mean (see Table 2.4). South Africa's capabilities in selected areas of technology, such as mining and civil engineering, railroad equipment and telecommunications, are impressive by world standards. Its hospitals, technical and scientific centres and universities are presently flooded with international staff, and 'in comparison to the rest of Africa and parts of the former Soviet empire and South East Asia, South Africa remains an attractive country: climatically, culturally, and economically'.[25] On the African continent, South Africa's manufacturing sector is nearly seven times larger than that of its nearest rival Nigeria (in terms of value added) and five times more than the combined total of the other SADC member countries. In 1996, its manufacturing output accounted for over 23 per cent of GDP, compared with 14 per cent in 1946. Indeed, as a whole, the share of the primary sector in GDP declined from 31.7 per cent in 1950 to 18.4 per cent in 1994, while the share of the secondary sector rose from 14.1 per cent to 28.5 per cent over the same period.[26] In 1992, the share of agriculture as a percentage of GDP was just 5 per cent, while manufacturing rose to 26 per cent.

With the exception of South Africa and Zimbabwe, the manufacturing sector contributed less than 15 per cent of GDP for most of the southern African countries in 1995. Furthermore, manufacturing activities involve mostly agricultural products (see Table 2.4).[27] Nearly all of their exports are in the form of primary products. In 1995, for instance, the SADC countries' total exports and imports (excluding South Africa and Mauritius) were estimated at US$103 billion and US$115 billion respectively. Mineral exports accounted for about 60 per cent and the remaining 40 per cent were made up of mostly agricultural commodities such as coffee, sugar, tea and tobacco.[28] Combined manufacturing exports in the SADC countries represent less than 20 per cent of regional exports, and less than 10 per cent if South Africa is excluded (see Table 2.5). In general, South Africa's visible exports to the rest of the region exceed imports by a factor of more than 5 : 1. Indeed, in 1996 South Africa exported $5583 million worth of manufactured goods. This was almost twice the value of manufactured exports by the rest of sub-Saharan Africa.[29] Its GNP per capita is three times that of the average for the other SADC states (only Mauritius has a higher GNP per capita), and is roughly

Table 2.4   SADC and South Africa – some salient statistics, 1996

	Area, sq. km (million)	*Population (millions)*	*Total GNP (US$m)*	*Per capita (US$m)*
Angola	1.25	9.40	8000	850
Botswana	0.58	1.20	1150	1000
Lesotho	0.03	1.67	690	410
Malawi	0.12	8.16	1320	160
Mozambique	0.80	15.00	1550	100
Namibia	0.82	1.66	1840	1100
Swaziland	0.02	0.74	540	790
Tanzania	0.95	24.74	3780	160
Zambia	0.75	7.49	2160	290
Zimbabwe	0.39	9.26	6070	660
SADC	5.71	79.32	26.560	335
South Africa	1.22	36.65	77.720	2120
Total	6.93	115.97	104.280	899
South Africa %	16.6	31.6	74.5	235.8

Source: SADC Annual Report, July 1992 – June 1993, Gaborone, 1993, p.11; ADB, *Economic Integration in Southern Africa*, Vol. 1, 1993, p. 376; World Bank, *World Development Report, 1989–1994*; IMF, *World Economic Outlook*, Washington DC, May 1995, p. 128.

three and a half times larger than that of the average for the COMESA and other SADC members combined.[30]

This picture of South Africa's regional dominance conceals the true tragedy of the region and, by extension, the continent's economic retrogression. While the South African economy is strong by African standards, it is nonetheless very small by global standards, and also ailing. During the last two or so decades, the fortunes of the South African economy have been rather mixed. Since the mid-1970s the South African economy has experienced a consistent decline in growth from 5.1 per cent per year during 1965–70 to 1.6 per cent during 1985–90, thus leading to a negative growth in per capita income during the 1980s. This declining growth performance has been coupled with a sharp decline in job creation. During the 1960s more than 80 per cent of the annual growth in the labour force found employment in the modern sectors of the economy; this ratio fell sharply to 26 per cent during 1980–85 and to 14.6 per cent during the subsequent five years. The figures for the latter part of the 1980s were positive, but below 2 per cent on average,[31] while in 1990–92 economic decline set in, continuing until 1993.[32]

In the early 1990s – partly as a response to the collapse of apartheid – the country witnessed an upswing in the economy, but this was merely a cyclical and temporary phenomenon.[33] Today, it is clear that the ensuing recovery from the early 1990s has been very uneven. Thus while the growth rate jumped to 6 per cent during the latter half of 1993,[34] it was only 1.5 per cent on an annual basis for that year. In 1993 it grew by 2.5 per cent rising to 3.5 per cent in 1995, but then fell to 3 per cent in 1996.[35] This relative improvement also conceals substantial fluctuations, with a decline of 1 per cent during the first half of 1994 followed by a 5.5 per cent expansion over the rest of the year.[36] There was then a somewhat steadier expansion of 3.5 per cent, 2.5 per cent, 3.5 per cent, 3 per cent and 3.5 per cent over the next six months to the end of 1996, and another dip to a mere 1 per cent during the first half of 1997.[37] With a population growth rate of around 2.2 per cent per year, the overall growth rates are not impressive. In per capita terms, the figure for 1994 is virtually negative and the following two years represent not more than 0.8–1.1 per cent per capita growth. Using the higher figure, it would take over fifty years to double per capita income in South Africa, while with the lower it would take over eighty years.

It is readily seen from this brief overview that the recent growth performance has been weak and uneven. Recorded growth rates have improved per capita income only marginally. In a situation where there are strong and repeated demands for substantial redistribution, such growth levels are far from sufficient. In spite of the fall of apartheid, South Africa remains a land of extreme socio-economic inequalities. In general the average black incomes are still one tenth of their white counterparts and the former's unemployment levels remain very high.

Unemployment

Under apartheid, the market acted like a malevolent invisible hand, working to the advantage of white workers and capitalists, and widening the wage differentials between whites and black workers. The ratio of per capita incomes of white to black people rose from 10.6 : 1 in 1946–47 to 15 : 1 in 1970.[38] White people comprised just 20 per cent of the population but earned about 70 per cent of the national income until the 1970s.[39] As the apartheid system unravelled, the black share of national income rose – from 20 per cent in 1970 to 25 per cent in 1980 and to almost 30 per cent in 1993. Racial discrimination in wages likewise declined dramatically. Yet the overall inter-

Table 2.5   SADC manufacturing exports – 1995 (US$ million)

Country	Total exports	Manufacturing exports	Manufactured as % of total
Angola	2 466	11	0.5
Botswana	1 479	38	2.6
Lesotho	54	16	19.6
Malawi	103	8	7.8
Mauritius	–	–	–
Namibia	947	44	4.7
Swaziland	469	58	12.4
Tanzania	402	73	18.2
Zambia	1 179	25	2.1
Zimbabwe	1 592	284	17.8
South Africa	21 549	4583	21.2
SADC total	30 532	5190	17.0

Source: Compiled from statistics from various sources.

household distribution of income in South Africa has not changed. Extreme inequality is still rooted in the labour market, but it is now driven to a large extent by rising unemployment.

Analysis of unemployment is beset by problems of conceptualization and measurement. Estimates of South Africa's unemployment rate have, for some time now, varied depending on the definition and data used in the calculation.[40] The unemployment rate is the number of unemployed people expressed as a percentage of the labour force. The measured rate thus depends on how the labour force is estimated, what counts as work and how unemployment is defined. Most reported unemployment refers to the standard recommended by the International Labour Organization (ILO): persons above a specific age who during the reference period are without work, are currently available for work and are seeking work. This makes unemployment hard to define partly because 'it combines a condition (being without work), a need (for work or for income), an attitude (desire for paid work), a capacity (ability to accept an opportunity, or at least be available to do so), and an activity (searching for work)'.[41]

Heavily influenced by the ILO, the Central Statistics Service (CSS) uses the following definition for unemployment in South Africa: those people within the economically active population who:

- did not work during the seven days prior to the interview;
- want to work and are available to start work within a week of interview; and
- have taken active steps to look for work or start some form of self-employment in the four weeks prior to the interview.

Table 2.6 indicates the official number of unemployed people in South Africa based on this definition from 1996 to 1998. The table also indicates the lower and upper limits of these estimates, using 95 per cent confidence intervals. The table shows that there has been an increase in both actual and proportional unemployment between 1996 and 1998. When comparing 1997 and 1998, the difference in unemployment rates using the official definition is not statistically significant, since there is an overlap in the confidence interval of the 1997 and 1998 estimates. The official unemployment in both years lies somewhere between 2 and 2.2 million. Although the actual number could lie somewhere between 3 and 4 million, the most

Table 2.6   Unemployment statistics

Unemployment	Estimate (000)	Lower limit (000)	Upper limit (000)	Unemployment rate (%)	Lower limit (%)	Upper limit (%)
1996	1698	1553	1735	16.9	16.1	17.7
1997	2019	1843	2196	21.0	19.4	22.6
1998	2238	2149	2328	22.9	22.1	23.7

Source: Central Statistics Service.

worrying factor about South Africa's unemployment figures is its racial dimension. The official unemployment rates for the different population groups ranged between 5 per cent for white people and 30 per cent for Africans (the African rate was more than six times as high as that for white people). At the extreme of the spectrum, one in every three (33 per cent) of all women of African origin was unemployed. At the other extreme, about one in every 30 (3 per cent) of white men are unemployed.

Crime

The rising rate of unemployment is also fostering a culture of crime. In 1995, only 10 per cent of South Africans viewed crime as the most pressing concern. This figure had nearly doubled by early 1997. In November 1998, over 22 per cent of South Africans placed crime as their top concern, just behind service delivery (24 per cent) and jobs (23 per cent). The most recent data indicate that crime has increased even further as a public priority. This is perhaps not surprising given recent statistical trends. Figures for the most common serious crime tendencies (all showing an annual incidence of more than twenty cases per 100 000 of the population per year) are compared for 1994, 1995, 1996 and 1998 in Table 2.7. An analysis of the figures pertaining to the crime tendencies featured in the table indicates that all categories under discussion have witnessed sustained increase since 1994. Rape, serious assault (assault and GBH), other robbery and the illegal possession of firearms continued to increase. Of these four, it is especially the increase in other robberies which is very significant. (However, it is worth noting that the overall incidence of robbery has declined because of a drastic decrease in the incidence of robbery

Table 2.7   Crime statistics – 1994, 1995, 1996 and 1998*

	1994	*1995*	*1996*	*1998*
Murder	66.6	64.6	61.1	66.8
Attempted murder	67.8	64.2	67.5	68.0
Robbery with aggravated assault	210.8	194.1	159.3	202.1
Rape	105.1	115.3	119.5	125.1
Assault	481.0	492.1	486.2	490.1
House-breaking	566.0	591.7	583.6	588.1
Theft – motor vehicle	258.9	245.2	229.4	267.1
Other theft	949.3	941.0	900	954.1
Drug related crime	117.0	98.9	92.9	109.1

*A comparison of the 1994, 1995, 1996 and 1998 increase/decrease in the crime ratio (per 100 000 of the population) related to specific crime categories.
Source: Crime Information Management Centre (CIMC).

with aggravating circumstances.) In the case of rape and the illegal possession of firearms the increase is still significant, but in the case of assault and GBH it is no longer really significant.

It is practically impossible to spend any time in South Africa without becoming directly or indirectly aware of the issue of crime. Of all the critical issues facing the new democracy, it is the only issue which seems to transcend all barriers and unite all the races – although for very different reasons. Many white South Africans regard crime as being essentially an activity carried out by certain of their black compatriots, and the fear of crime is used by white-led opposition parties and white journalists as a euphemism for fear of black rule, the traditional white South African fear of blacks (*swart gevaar*) in a new guise. Black township dwellers, who in fact are more likely to suffer crime than the people in suburbs, often blame the upsurge in crime on immigrants from elsewhere in Africa who have flocked to the country since the end of apartheid.

There is an element of truth in this. Apart from the growth of localized variants of organized crime, international organized crime groups have increasingly become active in South Africa. South Africa, in fact, has become Africa's capital of organized crime, with an estimated value of R41.5 billion per year. Criminals from abroad are attracted by the existence of a market for drugs and fraud, but equally important is the country's first-class transport infrastructure and banking system. South Africa is the world's tenth biggest stock exchange, which makes it an ideal base for intercontinental operations and money laundering. According to Mark Shaw of the Institute of Security Studies, the operations of the following groups constitute the greatest threat:[42]

- ***Nigerian organized crime groups***. The growth of Nigerian organized crime groups in South Africa over the last five years has been phenomenal. Organized crime assessments completed by the South African government indicate substantial activity by such groups in the country. Despite this, there have been comparatively few arrests and fewer successful prosecutions. Street-level drug officers in Johannesburg admit that they are largely unsuccessful in countering Nigerian and central African criminal organizations, and parts of inner city Johannesburg are increasingly dominated by the activities of Nigerian and central African 'drug lords'.[43]

- ***Russian Mafia***. Available information indicates that Russian citizens are involved in the activities of a number of criminal groups in several southern African states, particularly Angola, Botswana, Mozambique, Namibia, Swaziland and South Africa. The Russian Mafia groups concentrate mainly on diamond and weapon smuggling, corruption, fraud and money laundering schemes, as well as investment in legitimate business. For example, police intelligence reports show how Russian citizens residing in South Africa simultaneously have contacts in Mozambique to facilitate weapon smuggling to South Africa, while a private Russian business group is currently attempting to sell stockpiles of Russian armaments and ammunition to countries on the African continent. According to current information, an agency will be set up to facilitate the marketing and distribution of the weaponry. Officials in the Mozambican planning agency are reported to have close contacts with the Russian Mafia in South Africa.[44]

- ***Chinese Triads***. SAPS intelligence assessments argue that the growth of Chinese Triad activity in the country is closely related to the growing number of Chinese illegal immigrants entering the country. Triads in particular have been involved in the smuggling of endangered species or products derived from such species. Recent police operations in the Western Cape have reaped some benefit. Various Chinese criminal syndicates have been uncovered and some leaders and members apprehended in connection with a variety of crimes ranging from abalone smuggling, prostitution, murder, blackmail and the possession of unlicensed firearms. Almost unprecedented arrays of state policing agencies were involved in the investigations. These included, among others, the Western Cape Organized Crime Investigation Unit, SANAB, SAPS Internal Security, the Illegal Immigration Investigation Unit, the Endangered Species Protection Unit and the Department of Sea Fisheries. (The diversity of agencies engaged in the investigation of organized crime and the problems associated with this is discussed below.)

The South African Police Service (SAPS), demoralized and ill prepared for the transition to democratic rule, often appears overwhelmed with the upsurge in organized crime. Police spokesmen even admit that elements of the force have themselves been penetrated by organized crime. Given the history of South Africa's Police Service, this is perhaps not surprising. For decades the police concentrated so single-mindedly on the threat of communist subversion that it ignored the deep changes taking place in the political economy of crime in southern Africa.

For the wider South African society, although the high level of crime affects all, its impacts and its effects appear to vary between racial groups. For affluent, suburban whites, growing evidence suggests that it is the prime threat to confidence in the new order and the factor most likely to prompt continued emigration among a sector of the society whose mobility is high and whose commitment to majority rule is conditional.[45] Since skills and resources are disproportionately concentrated in this group, its flight from attacks on persons and property would weaken the democracy's economic foundation. There is also evidence that predominantly white residents of the suburbs may react to crime by seeking to insulate themselves physically from the mainly black poor who are seen as its perpetrators. That would entrench a form of social distance which will impede attempts to create a common South African loyalty.[46] For much of the black majority, exit is neither a feasible nor a desired option. And, since this section of society has been living with high rates of violent crime for decades, concern at a relative increase is far outweighed by enthusiasm for a new order in which black people are full citizens. There is, as yet, no visible evidence that crime is substantially denting black confidence in democracy. In addition, recent research suggests that black citizens see crime as a symptom of social and economic inequalities rather than as a product of democracy's 'weakness'.[47] Survey results suggest that white and black citizens view increasing crime and state responses from diametrically opposed positions: whites see crime as a breakdown of policing standards and the weakness of the new order; blacks view increasing lawlessness as a sign that the new democracy has not been consolidated and that its institutions need strengthening.

AIDS

At the end of the 1990s, the World Health Organization estimated that there were 8–10 million people in the world afflicted with the AIDS virus. Sub-Saharan Africa, with only 10 per cent of the world's population, had 25–50 per cent of AIDS-infected population.[48] During the 1994 conference in Morocco, the WHO upped the estimated infected population to over 15 million. The largest number of new cases was in Africa – with more than 1.5 million. This brings the total in Africa to 10 million (WHO press release, October 1999). In 1999, the number of people with HIV worldwide has reportedly increased again – to 19.1 million, with 44 per cent of new infections (2.3 million) in sub-Saharan Africa. Almost two-thirds of the HIV infections occur in the under-25 age group. The mode of infection is heterosexual, and in some locations HIV rates are five times higher among girls than among boys between the ages of 15 and 19.

The impact of HIV/AIDS is broad and multifaceted. Overall, at this time, the greatest impact is at the micro (household) level, but it is progressing towards the macro (national) level.

- Initially those who are HIV/AIDS positive have to deal with the stigma of infection and subsequent disease, which not only affects friendships and familial relationships, but also makes it difficult or impossible to obtain employment.
- Because of the heterosexual transmission, there is a strong likelihood of both husband and wife dying, leaving increasing numbers of orphans. This may have a further impact on the children's standard of living and chances for education, and it will place an

increased burden on the family members who absorb them into their households.

- As the number of infected women increases, the percentage of children born HIV positive will increase, and the child mortality rate will increase.
- The largest number of AIDS cases tends to be among men and women in the most productive age groups. As the disease continues to spread, it could have a profound impact on the supply of labour, reducing the size and productivity of the labour force, including the highly trained sector.
- In the rural areas, there may be a reduction in the number of adults who can produce food, and there may be a significant change in the gender-based division of labour on the farm.

The ultimate demographic impact of AIDS is uncertain, but what is certainly known is alarming. For example, in 1993 Ethiopia reported a half-million cases of HIV/AIDS. In many Nigerian clinics that treat sexually transmitted diseases, up to 22 per cent of men have the virus. In Francistown, Botswana, a third of women seeking antenatal care are HIV infected (WHO). AIDS is now the leading cause of death for adolescent males and the second leading cause of death for adolescent females in the Côte d'Ivoire.

Although central and eastern Africa are most affected by AIDS, the rate of infection is rising throughout the continent. South Africa represents one of the regions with the fastest rate of HIV infection on the continent.[49] National Sentinel surveillance surveys of antenatal clinic attendees have been conducted in South Africa since 1990, and HIV information is available by state. In Natal and Western, Eastern and Gauteng States where the major urban areas of Johannesburg, Pretoria, Durban and Port Elizabeth are located, HIV prevalence among antenatal clinic attendees tested increased from less than 1 per cent in 1990 to a median of 15 per cent in 1997.[50] In 1997 HIV prevalence ranged from 6 to 27 per cent. Age detail is available for the years 1992 to 1995. HIV prevalence among antenatal clinic attendees less than 20 years of age increased from 2 per cent in 1991 to 9 per cent in 1995. Peak HIV infection occurred among antenatal clinic attendees 20 to 24 years of age. In this age group, HIV prevalence increased from 3 to 14 per cent.[51] In Free, North Cape, Mpumalanga, Northern and North West States, HIV prevalence among antenatal clinic attendees tested increased from less than 1 per cent in 1990 to 20 per cent in 1997. In 1997 HIV prevalence ranged from 8 to 25 per cent. Age detail is available for the years 1991 to 1995.[52] HIV prevalence among antenatal clinic attendees less than 20 years of age increased from less than 1 per cent to 4 per cent. Peak HIV prevalence occurred among women aged 20 to 29 years of age. There is no information available on HIV prevalence among sex workers in South Africa.

Over the next three years, the annual death toll is expected to be 200 000, leaving behind almost 600 000 AIDS-infected orphans in South Africa. The WHO calculates that the epidemic will peak between 2005 and 2010, with 6 million people infected and some 600 000 of them contracting full-blown AIDS – with the greatest impact among 30 to 40 year olds. The disease is projected to cut average life expectancy by some 20 years and to shrink economic growth in South Africa by 2 per cent.[53] Both the full economic and human consequences of AIDS are still to be seen and the reintegration process itself may not survive such a shock. Existing stress, now being addressed at the national level, will be exacerbated to unmanageable levels by the cumulative impact of AIDS-related mortality (see pp. 125–31 below).

Conclusion

Everything about modern South Africa is about race. Race is spoken about overtly and often in terms of the country's diverse demographics: 77 per cent black; 11 per cent white; 9 per cent mixed-raced, known as coloured; and 3 per cent Indian. At a still deeper level, the dynamics of race are here signalled subliminally. Code words and symbols take the place of a difficult discourse on issues such as how to redress the ravages of apartheid, and how to accord blacks greater access to the nation's wealth and influence over the economy, academia and other sectors still dominated by whites. As the country proceeds beyond its second multi-party elections, the economy, unemployment, crime and AIDS have all emerged as critical issues inducing insecurity in all the diverse races in the Republic.

3
Regionalization, Integration and Southern Africa

The growing struggle for world markets, increasing protectionism, clashes over monetary and debt issues as well as changing security concerns of states are all signs of a changing global economic order. Increasingly, this order is characterized by segmentation and composed of regional blocs. This chapter begins by reviewing the concept of regionalism, then moves to contextualize its normative appeal for southern African states. It concludes by highlighting the limits to regionalism in southern Africa.

Integration and regionalization

The global political economy at the dawn of the twenty-first century seems to be pulled in two opposite directions. One force, nationalism, is seemingly tearing apart nations that, for much of the twentieth century, have been part of stable political entities.[1] The human suffering which underlies it, as well as its impact on regional peace and security, has brought into sharp focus the ways in which different categories of people are marginal to the states in which they live and the various forms of insecurity confronting them.[2] In parallel with nationalism, the seemingly irresistible force of integration is binding different nations together and creating supra-state alliances.[3] Although the motivations for these alliances are many, the driving force remains firmly economic. Not surprisingly the trend is often referred to as economic integration (unifying the economic structures of a group of nations).

From the literature it is unclear what the concept actually means. Does the concept only apply, for example, to the end result of the process, or to both the process and the end result? Amitai Etzioni, for instance, defines integration as a self-sustaining mechanism that helps a community to maintain itself, its existence and its form by its 'own processes' without having to depend on external processes of its member units.[4] From this basis he attributes three strands of integration to a political community. These are that (a) it has an effective control over the use of the means of violence, (b) it has a centre of decision-making that is able to affect significantly the allocation of resources and rewards through the community, and (c) it is the dominant form of political identification for a large majority of politically aware citizens.[5] From this perspective, integration is treated as an end result and not as a process.

Deutsch on the other hand, sees integration as a process. In an influential study in 1988, he sums up the goals of integration as: maintaining peace, attaining peace, accomplishing some specific tasks, and gaining a new image and role identity. The process, according to Deutsch, leads either to an amalgamated or a pluralistic security community depending on the main goals.[6] In a similar manner, Haas provides a working definition of integration as 'a process for the creation of political communities described in institutional and attitudinal terms'.[7] These definitional differences are by no means exhaustive. The point is further exacerbated by a lack of conceptual clarity about the dependent variables. This gives rise to difficulties in relating the concepts of different scholars. Hence, this has the consequence that integration theorists tend to 'talk past each other'. Even in instances where theorists have confronted each other, the differences in conceptualization have made the resolution of these differences unnecessarily difficult. Such differences in conceptualization makes comparison of different regional integration processes difficult.

One possible exception to this conceptual malaise is the recent work of Björn Hettne. In exploring the significance of the current integrative process for global order and security, Hettne applies in an original manner the ideas of Karl Polanyi (who wrote his major works during the Second World War) to the recent developments in the global economy and polity. Hettne thinks that we are experiencing a Second Great Transformation that is characterized by a double-movement: on the one hand continuing market expansion with globalization which, conversely, provokes a reactive force of rising regionalism. According to Hettne this flexibility in scope and intensity is largely a product of late modernity. In his words, it 'constitutes a new form of regionalism'. Unlike the 'old' preoccupation of regional bodies with economic integration, the 'new' regionalism is largely a political response to the market-driven process of globalization and the social eruptions associated with this process.[8] Globalization as used here refers broadly to the processes whereby power is located in global social formations and expressed through global networks rather than through territorially based states.

In this context, the process of globalization is driven by capitalism, which has entered a stage wherein accumulation is taking place on a global rather than a national scale. This process of globalization has been accelerating with the restructuring of the global capitalist economy since the demise of the Bretton Woods system in the early 1970s. Deepening inequalities have resulted from this process over the 1970s and 1980s. While current developments in global capitalism are affording untold wealth and luxury for significant strata of the world's population, this is being achieved at the expense of others. This global tendency of redistribution of resources from South to North, and from poor to rich is especially acute in Africa (a point to which I shall return).

The new regionalism is composed of economic, political, social and cultural aspects that go far beyond traditional or economic preoccupation with markets and free trade arrangements. Rather, the political ambition of establishing regional coherence and regional identity, apart from security and welfare, seems to be of primary importance. In Hettne's typology, there are five generalized levels or stages of 'regionness' which may be said to define the structural position of a particular region in terms of regional coherence. The first stage he called the *geographical unit*. These geographical units are delimited by more or less natural physical barriers and marked by ecological characteristics: 'Europe from the Atlantic to the Urals', 'Africa South of the Sahara', 'Central Asia', or 'the Indian subcontinent'. This first level can be referred to as a 'proto-region', or a 'preregional zone', since there is no organized international society. To further regionalize, this particular territory must, necessarily, be inhabited by human beings, maintaining some kind of translocal relationship.[9] This brings us to the second dimension or what he calls *social systems*.

This stage implies ever-widening translocal relations between human groups. Such relations of embryonic interdependence constitute a 'security complex', in which the constituent units, as far as their own security is concerned, are dependent on each other as well as on the overall stability of the regional system. The region, just like the larger international system of which it forms part, can therefore on this level of regionness be described as anarchic. The classic case of such a regional order is nineteenth-century Europe. At this low level of regionness, a balance of power, or some kind of 'concert', is the sole security guarantee. This is a rather primitive security mechanism. Similarly, the exchange system tends to be based on symbolic kinship bonds rather than trust. We could therefore talk of a 'primitive' region, exemplified, as far as security is concerned, by East Asia (in spite of a high degree of spontaneous economic integration) or the Balkans today.

The third stage is *transnational cooperation*, organized or more spontaneous and informal, in any of the cultural, economic, political or military fields or in several of them at the same time (multidimensional regionalization). In the case of more organized cooperation, region is defined by the list of countries which are the formal members of the regional organization in question. The more organized region could be called the 'formal' region. In order to assess the relevance and future potential of a particular regional organization, it should be possible to relate the 'formal region' (defined by organizational membership) to the 'real region', which has to be defined in terms of potentialities and convergences and through other less precise criteria. This is the stage where the crucial regionalization process takes place. This process can be described as a convergence along several economic, political and cultural dimensions.

Stage four occurs when *civil society* takes shape through an enduring organizational framework (formal or less formal) to facilitate and promote social communication and convergence of values and actions throughout the region. Of course the pre-existence of a shared cultural tradition (an inherent regional civil society) in a particular region is of crucial importance, particularly for more informal forms of regional cooperation, but it must be remembered that culture is not only a given, but continuously created and recreated. However, the defining element here is the multidimensional and voluntary quality of regional cooperation, and the societal characteristics indicating an emerging 'regional anarchic society', that is, something more than anarchy, but still less than society. In security terms the reference is to 'security community'.

The final stage is reached when the region assumes a *personality* with a distinct identity, actor capability, legitimacy and structure of decision-making. Crucial areas for regional intervention are organized conflict resolution (between and particularly within former 'states') and creation of welfare (in terms of social security and regional balance). This process is similar to state-formation and nation-building, and the ultimate outcome could be a 'region-state', which in terms of scope and cultural heterogeneity can be compared to the classical empires, but in terms of political order constitutes a voluntary evolution of a group of formerly sovereign national, political units into a supra-national security community, where sovereignty is pooled for the good of all. This is basically the idea of the European Union as outlined in the treaty of Maastricht. The gap between idea and reality is still very big. Thus region in this sense is still something for the future, particularly outside Europe. It should be emphasized that conflict resolution in order to properly reflect this stage, implies the existence of institutions and mechanisms, not *ad hoc* interventions of the type that happen today. However, these attempts at crisis management underline the need for more institutional forms of conflict resolution at the regional level.

Hettne is quick to reassure us that his five levels or stages, while displaying signs of an evolutionary logic, are nonetheless non-deterministic. This is important, not least because it emphasizes the fluidity of the integration process and also the critico-reflective potential of the forces driving the process forward. In this sense, there is a great deal to admire in Hettne's work. For the analyst, it implies that the act of constitution (the co-constitution of people and society) makes history, while also asserting that social construction is a contingent effect of political practices within history. Such a claim can also be conceived as part of a wider effort to transcend the dichotomy between objectivism and relativism in contemporary social research by developing a notion of human rationality as practical but critical reason or wisdom.[10] By rejecting the subject/object dichotomy and embedding the analyst, and indeed all human agents and subjects, in the co-constitution of history, Hettne's typology opens up a rapprochement between philosophy and ontology or theories about the making of social worlds and histories, and with these the making of being-in-the-world.

Regionalism and southern Africa

Until recently the shadow of apartheid undermined any genuine attempt to create a southern African community that incorporated South Africa and extended beyond Botswana, Lesotho and Swaziland.[11] Consequently, the most striking feature of the region's politico-economic landscape is its division into competing alliances. Furthermore, the importance attached to economic relations in the region's conflicts made the behaviour and success of these alliances difficult.[12] In the last decade of the twentieth century, the region stands at the threshold of a new era.[13] Once torn by ideological conflicts and the dominance of command economies, the region is now moving towards economic liberalization and openness. Structural adjustment of one sort or another is being attempted simultaneously in virtually all the region's economies. In general, the ascendancy of 'market economics' is acknowledged by its governments albeit with different degrees of enthusiasm.

These developments have generated a climate of hope for further beneficial changes in the region. In particular, the desirability of greater regionalism along economic lines[14] has become an item of faith among large segments of the political and intellectual elites of the region.[15] In the wider international community the idea is reflexively chanted as a mantra by means of which the region's economic woes would be ameliorated and the prospects of socio-political stability vastly improved.[16] In the words of the World Bank: 'it is reasonable to assume that solutions will be found to the problems that have divided the people of that region [southern Africa] and that South African economic cooperation will eventually transform the prospects for the whole of southern Africa.'[17] More generally, the Bank has now made regional integration a priority. In a policy document the Bank concludes that 'progress towards market integration and increased cooperation in a whole range of areas – economic, technical, environmental, food security, education, and research – is central to Africa's long term development strategy.'[18]

Unlike Hettne's political typology, the form of regionalism envisaged for the subcontinent is indebted to the philosophical and methodological insights of classical economics. In the economics literature it is referred to as customs union theory. Jacob Viner[19] and James Meade[20] are often credited with founding the theory of customs union. It was, however, Bela Belassa who gave the theory its practical context.[21] In 1961 Bela Belassa interpreted customs union theory as an evolutionary process comprising four successive stages with each stage involving more complex and higher levels of integration. These are as follows:

- At the lowest level there is a free trade area in which tariffs and quotas are eliminated among members.
- A customs union goes a stage further. In addition to the elimination of internal quotas, a customs union erects common external tariffs.
- The next level is a common market, which combines the features of the customs union with the elimination of barriers against the free movement of labour and capital.
- The fourth stage is economic union or community. Beyond the features of a common market, an economic union harmonizes economic policies among members and sometimes adopts a common currency.

A *free trade area* (FTA) involves a relatively minimal degree of integration. Nations in an FTA agree to eliminate tariff barriers to trade for goods and services they produce themselves. Each nation, however, retains the right to set its own tariff barriers with respect to produce from outside the FTA. The fact that some goods are tariff-free in FTA transactions, while other goods are still subject to differential trade barriers, complicates intra-FTA trade and therefore limits the effective degree of integration. The North American Free Trade Area (NAFTA) represents the most advanced FTA system in the world. Here goods from member states (the United States, Canada and Mexico) are traded freely within their borders. Goods from other countries, however, are subjected to the differential tariff barriers of the member states.

The next level of economic integration is called a *customs union*. (Customs is another word for a tariff.) Under a customs union, a group of countries agree to tariff-free trade within their collective borders and to a common set of external trade barriers. If NAFTA were to evolve into a customs union, for example, the United States, Canada and Mexico would need to agree to a unified set of tariff barriers that would apply to products from other countries. The Treaty of Rome, which eventually led to the modern European Union, was based upon the idea of customs union.

The movement to a common market is an important step in terms of economic and political integration. The countries involved give up some degree of their sovereignty or national political power, since they can no longer set their own trade barriers without consulting their economic partners. What they gain from the process is a far greater degree of economic integration. Products flow more easily within a customs union, with no need for border inspections or customs fees because of the unified trade structure. In practice, of course, the elimination of trade barriers is not as complete as the theory suggests, since member states retain the right to impose some non-tariff trade barriers, such as health and safety standards, for example.

An economic union is the final stage of economic and political integration. In an economic union, non-tariff barriers are eliminated along with tariff barriers, creating an even more fully integrated market. The degree of integration in an economic union goes further than this, however. Members of an economic union agree to four 'freedoms' of movement: of goods, services, people and capital. These four freedoms represent significant limitations on national sovereignty, but they can also have significant effects on economic activity. The freedom of movement of goods is more complicated than it may seem, as it goes beyond the elimination of tariff barriers. Free movement of goods requires a variety of governmental health, safety and other standards and regulations to be 'harmonized' so that, at least in theory, a product that can be sold somewhere in the economic union can, in fact, be sold everywhere in it. Freedom of movement is also more complicated than it may seem. The service sector of international trade includes many industries, such as banking and finance, traditionally subject to heavy regulation that varies considerably among nations. Freedom of movement of people requires a unified immigration policy, since a person free to enter and work in one member state of the economic union would, in theory, be able to live and work anywhere in the area.

For southern Africa, it is hoped that economic integration can yield greater developmental benefit by collective rather than unilateral use of certain economic policies and instruments. The perceived advantage for the subcontinent of Africa falls into two broad categories: (a) *efficiency gains* in markets which arise from overcoming the functional losses in allocative, administrative and transaction costs associated with (i) small market size, (ii) market distortion and (iii) barriers to the movement of productive factors as well as goods/services resulting from productive national policies;[22] (b) *scale gains* in major project investments that result from large cost savings realized as a result of regionally coordinated developmental investment in physical, social and institutional infrastructure. Efficiency gains from regional integration usually occur (and occur first to the private sector) as a result of market-based trade liberalization which rationalizes national economic structures, achieves an expansion of output and trade within the region, expands and rationalizes investment flows, and integrates production to achieve scale economies. Scale gains occur mainly from public savings resulting from rationalization of investments in power generation, transmission and distribution, road systems, rail networks, airline systems, airport management and investments in health care and educational facilities. Regional economic integration might, by stimulating the supply-response of SAR economies, also accelerate the process of successful structural adjustment in SAR. That outcome remains elusive after a decade of intense adjustment pressures.

In addition, there are other kinds of possible gains that need to be recognized as well. These include externalities such as: improvements in production techniques to lower costs; decreases in rent-seeking elements in mark-ups in protected national markets; greater product range and diversity in regional production; and production rationalization and specialization in large, efficient plants. Integration may also make the region as a whole more attractive to foreign investment for the production of consumer durables than would fragmented national economies. Regional market integration in SAR could also foster greater competitiveness in the operation of firms which produce and distribute goods and which support those key functions. Improved policy coordination as a feature of regional integration could also yield overall welfare gains if policies which are now nationally controlled (e.g. the exchange rate of the rand in SAR's or the RSA's labour market policies) were to be modified with their regional repercussions in mind.

Limits to regionalism in southern Africa

If there is anywhere in sub-Saharan Africa where the continental drift towards economic collapse is not merely avoidable but also reversible, it is surely in southern Africa. By comparison to the rest of the continent, the region is well endowed with resources, both natural and human, and – the ravages of war and apartheid notwithstanding – much of the basic economic infrastructure remains sound or capable of early rehabilitation. There are, however, many obstacles in the way of transforming the region's assets into tangible integrative strategies. Three in particular are worthy of further attention. These are: (a) the inappropriateness of the model of integration chosen; (b) the role of South Africa; and (c) the absence of peace in a number of regional states.

The appropriateness of customs union

Customs union theory makes the same basic assumptions as the static theory of comparative advantage.[23] It thus deals with a situation in which input of factors of production, the state of technical knowledge, tests and forms of economic organization are all treated as constant or autonomous variables.[24] Trade within each country is assumed to be perfectly competitive; full employment is applied and the problems of adjustment in connection with the formation of a customs union are disregarded. This is a far cry from reality, and as Robson astutely observed: 'they do not apply in the advanced market economies, on the basis of which the theory was developed, and they apply even less in the underdeveloped economies of Africa.'[25]

Most data show that compared to other regions African countries have a very divergent pattern of industrialization. There is a corresponding variability in individual countries' participation in total intra-group trade. This huge imbalance in trade and industrialization in Africa has two implications for trade integration. First, it benefits disproportionately those countries that happen to have the greatest share of industrial output and intra-regional trade. Second, it justifiably raises concerns among the poorest countries that removal of barriers to trade may cause the migration of the few industries they possess to the industrially more advanced countries, thereby polarizing even further the existing uneven patterns of industrial development.[26]

Elsewhere, Mytelka has argued cogently that regional integration in developing countries will fail unless the problem of unequal gains is solved.[27] While perhaps she overstates her case in asserting that integration enjoys no legitimacy other than its ability to contribute towards the attainment of national economic development goals, the political capital favourable to integration arising from African aspirations for regional and continental unity is soon exhausted unless the distribution is effectively resolved.[28] For southern African politicians, beset by such domestic problems as high unemployment, acute poverty and demand expectations which have been exacerbated by the rhetoric of political necessity, cannot afford to sacrifice domestic economic growth for regional cooperation without inviting swift overthrow. Unfortunately, this dilemma applies as much to those that are gaining disproportionately from regional integration as to those that are less fortunate. In the poverty of the southern African situation even the relatively prosperous cannot afford – economically and politically – to make sacrifices on behalf of their weaker brethren. Loss of foreign investment or a single manufacturing concern to a neighbouring state has serious consequences for local employment, balance of payments and domestic political support.

This is patently obvious when we analyse the experience with attempts at economic integration in other parts of the African continent. Here we find that political leaders are deeply concerned that, in a situation of open markets and free enterprise, the gains of member states will be related positively to the degree of their economic development. Hence, for example, Nigeria, Kenya, Egypt, Zimbabwe and South Africa are regarded by many to possess an unfair advantage in potential unions. Indeed, the fears about the so-called 'backwash effect' whereby the more advanced in any grouping not only capture all the economic gains, but in fact do so at the expense of the less developed economies, is not without foundation.[29] Examples, if any were needed, are littered across the continent. The break-up of the East African Community towards the end of the 1970s was, in part, due to the fact that Tanzania felt that Kenya's industrialization was greatly helped by the Community and that its own was not. An attempt to use differential intra-union tariffs – designed to 'transfer taxes' – could not alleviate the problem, at least not to the satisfaction of Tanzania. On the positive side, it needs to be noted that the Communauté Economique de l'Afrique de l'Ouest (CEAO) has been more successful in its attempt to compensate the other members of the union for their 'assistance' in the industrial development of Côte d'Ivoire and Senegal. Tax revenues from imports enabled the Fonds Communautaires de Développement (FCD) to be created in 1976,[30] followed by the Fonds de Solidarité et d'Intervention pour le Développement de la Communauté in 1978. Moreover, the governments concerned do not appear averse to differential intra-union tariffs to assist the less developed members of the CEAO. For instance, they have instituted the system known as *taxes de co-opération régionale*, which can vary by product, by enterprise and by country. But it is doubtful that all these special arrangements are sustainable, especially as the two major contributors to the FCD, Senegal and Côte d'Ivoire, might be faced with financial difficulties or serious constraints for some years to come.[31]

South African regional dominance

Without traversing the corpus of literature on South African hegemony, it is worth noting that, with the exceptions of Angola and Tanzania, South African capital has been the primary source of investment for the rest of the SADC region. The premier position of South Africa in the region gives it a dominant role in controlling the structures of regional finance and credit. In Zimbabwe, for example, an estimated 25–30 per cent of privately owned capital stock is reckoned to be South African, although there has been a small reduction since 1990. It is estimated that South Africans own approximately 40 per cent of registered industrial enterprises in Botswana. In Zambia, South Africa owns key mining engineering firms and dominates the freight and forwarding business throughout the region.[32]

Political normalization in the wake of the demise of apartheid has led to a rapid increase in exports to the region, but imports from the region remain low to negligible, widening the gap in visible exports between South Africa and its neighbours.[33] South African exports to SADC countries, mainly value-added goods, increased by 30 per cent between 1996 and 1997 and the figures are higher than exports to the European Union, traditionally the country's biggest trading partner. Yet imports from SADC neighbours accounted for only 5 per cent of South African imports,[34] a clearly untenable situation in view of the fact that the benefits of economic interaction accrue mostly to South Africa, reinforcing historical asymmetries and distrust of the country. Advocating customs union theory will not reduce polarization as the 'invisible hand of the market' does not spread benefits equally, but relatively. From a study conducted in 1995 it transpired that South Africa would benefit most from liberalization and that at least four SADC countries would experience a net negative impact on their GDP.[35]

In general, the SADC members' imports to South Africa are concentrated in primary, mostly agricultural goods, competition for which among the region's nations is not likely to be lessened, and thus the terms of trade would consistently favour South Africa, unless South Africa was willing to institute a compensatory policy along the lines of the European Union's Common Agricultural Policy (CAP) for southern African farmers. In the short term, this is highly unlikely given South Africa's own budgetary crisis and development needs and her desire to control unemployment. Furthermore, in view of South Africa's highly developed infrastructure, most foreign investors are likely to select that country as their first choice for establishing plants. Thus South Africa would have no incentive to restrict growth within its own borders in order to nurture infant industries in the rest of the region except where they are 'branch plants' or support the industrialization needs of South Africa.

This is not a deleterious argument. It is based on historical evidence of relations among countries with unequal bargaining power, resource dependency and varying levels of existing economic development. Indeed, given the fundamental mismatch between South Africa's import profile and what the region is currently exporting, the critical question becomes whether southern African countries can transform their economies so that they are more than mere raw material producers and actually make products that South Africa will buy. In reality, South Africa has very little need for these raw materials. What it needs in terms of raw materials it probably buys already, suggesting that the immediate scope for increased regional exports to Southern Africa will mainly be a function of economic growth rather than increased market share. Thus prospects for increased exports from the region to South Africa, which would be an important component of any regional economic resurgence, hinge far less on the transition in South Africa than on the success of economic reforms in the countries of the region.

Given the transformation required, there is little hope that any of the countries in the region except for Zimbabwe will soon develop new industries that could count South Africa, among other places, as a significant market. Accordingly, in contrast to much of the literature, the critical variable, at least for inter-regional trade, is not the attitude of South Africa towards the region but the decisions made by the leaders of the other countries. A further problem, and one with political implications, is that increased economic growth in South Africa or perceived greater opportunities in South Africa may also cause labour from across the region to concentrate in South Africa. The whole issue of labour migration, particularly illegal migrants, is already a sensitive issue in the region and one with the potential to cause conflict among various states,[36] both those who feel they cannot host large numbers of economic migrants (South Africa, and to some extent Namibia and Botswana) and those who feel that they suffer from brain drain (Zimbabwe and Mozambique) due to the more attractive prospects offered by the more advanced economies in the region. It is telling that SADC has been attempting to finalize a protocol on the free movement of people ever since 1995, but that no consensus has as yet been reached on this sensitive issue.

Two principle consequences for regional systems result from this asymmetrical interdependence between South Africa and other regional states. First, regional arrangements may be subject to considerable strain as a result of changes induced in the economies of partner states by South African pressure. The collapse of the price of a key commodity, the contraction of export markets or inflation in the South African economy may weaken the economies of partner states to such an extent that it is difficult for them to continue to fulfil regional commitments. In order to economize on scarce foreign exchange there is a great temptation to place national before regional interests and to curtail regional interactions. Second, in a situation of asymmetrical interdependence, arrangements with extra-regional actors may appear more attractive than those with neighbouring states. Such actors are better able to provide what South Africa seeks in the way of development prerequisites. Arrangements with developed states or multinational corporations may be made even if these conflict with, and undermine, regional goals, and despite the fact that the individual state may be in a weaker bargaining position than if the regional partners negotiated on a joint basis.

Regional peace

The third major constraint on regionalization in southern Africa is the absence of intra-state peace, rooted in a lack of political cohesion, the spill-over effects of civil war and upheaval into neighbouring countries and the involvement of external (neighbouring) powers in internal conflicts.[37] The extent to which domestic politics and other dynamics impact on regionalization seems to be an issue that is largely neglected in scholarly work on the topic. The tendency to ignore the internal dimension and concentrate on inter-state relations in the process of regionalization is still alive and well. Deutsch and his colleagues identified the existence of peaceful relations and the expectation that this state of affairs would continue for the foreseeable future as one of the major requirements (and a strong impetus) for the development of a security community. Adler remarks that one of the primary conditions for the existence of peace is 'a higher expected utility from peace than war'.[38] These authors, though, are clearly referring to international relations. In the southern African context it is becoming tragically clear that in a number of states, particularly Angola, there is not as yet any sense or conviction that peace, rather than war, has a higher utility. Rather, it would seem that one of the major reasons, if not the main reason, for Savimbi continuing the Angolan civil war is exactly the fact that what he (and by extension Unita) will gain from peace is not as much as what they are gaining from war. Unita's control of certain lucrative sectors of the Angolan economy and its agreements and deals with external business actors are too valuable to relinquish. Furthermore, these actors would seem to supply Savimbi with the means to continue his defiance of the international community (the UN). The point is that such incidences of continued internal strife and war pose serious obstacles to regionalization. There is little agreement within SADC on how to contribute towards peace in Angola and there is a serious lack of confidence and trust among the various states when it comes to the issue.

The Democratic Republic of Congo crisis illustrates a number of problems related to regionalization in southern Africa, and points to the limits to this process. The first is that regionalization is usually an attempt to find an optimum size for the efficient performance of certain tasks, 'judged crucial . . . for the advantage of governments'.[39] Although Taylor uses these words in the context of regionalism as a utilitarian concept, referring to 'functions' and the functionalist approach to regionalization, the benefits of the process may also encompass security and development cooperation for the benefit of the region's members. The bottom line remains that of the scale of the political, economic and geographical area best fitted for realizing these objectives. A region that is expanding continuously without assessment of the costs involved in such expansion (the process is, after all, aimed at increasing *benefits*) may become dysfunctional at worst, or little more than of symbolic value and meaning. Membership as 'reward' is a dubious criterion for enlargement and in this case southern Africa might do well by following the example of the European Union and study and debate enlargement beforehand. Unless the costs and benefits of expansion, in economic, political and security terms, are well understood, provided for or 'affordable' to the region, expansion might hamper or seriously damage regionalization. This may happen not only in terms of direct economic costs, but also indirectly, e.g. via the cost of military involvement by other members, the political risk of becoming embroiled in a conflict in which extra-regional entities may also have a stake and the potential for friction and conflict between members as a result of differences about the approach to newcomers to be followed.

4
Regionalism through Institutions: SACU, SADC and COMESA

At present, there exists a multiplicity of institutional arrangements for facilitating cooperation of various types and involving different degrees of intensity at the sector, institutional and project levels. Principal among these are: the Southern African Development Community (SADC), the Southern African Customs Union (SACU) and the Common Market for Eastern and Southern Africa (COMESA). If the vision of a subcontinental community is truly to be achieved, then it is essential to focus our attention on the available options for moving these crucial institutions from their current positions towards less fragmented arrangements for promoting subregional integration. In what follows, this chapter reviews the positions of these historical institutions and speculates on their transformative potentials.

The Southern African Customs Union

SACU is the oldest integrative arrangement in southern Africa and for that matter the continent. It was established in 1889, and by 1895 it had grown to cover the entire area of what are today South Africa, Botswana, Lesotho, Swaziland and Namibia (BLSN).[1] SACU provides for the duty-free movement of goods and services between member states and also for a common external tariff against the rest of the world, but also goes beyond a purely customs union in that it includes excise duties as well. In its Preamble, SACU's objectives are stated as:

> to ensure the continued economic development of the customs union area as a whole, and to ensure in particular that these

arrangements encourage the development of the less advanced members of the customs union and the diversification of their economies and afford to all parties equitable benefits arising from trade among themselves and with other countries.

To moderate South Africa's regional dominance, there is a compensation mechanism or – in the jargon a revenue-sharing formula with compensation factor – of 42 per cent for BLSN. The amount so calculated is then amended by a stabilization factor aimed at guaranteeing to each BLSN country a rate of revenue of between 17 and 23 per cent.[2] The Customs Union Commission meets annually, but SACU has no office or staff: it is handled by government departments in each member state while the common revenue pool is managed by the South African Reserve Bank.[3] Until 1976 – when Botswana withdrew – all five were also members of the Common (or Rand) Monetary Area (CMA). For historical reasons an important feature of SACU is that no member state may enter into a concessionary trade agreement with an outside country unless its partners agree.

In the context of providing economic stability to the smaller BLS members, contributing to their steady development and growth, maintaining a relatively stable currency regime and enabling their access to a wide range of goods and services, SACU has been successful in meeting its key objectives. At the very least its existence has not hindered the development of BLS to a degree which has retarded their growth and development in any significant way. In general, real per capita income increased in each of the BLS countries over the 1980s. Formal sector employment in the BLS countries has grown although, with the exception of Botswana, such growth has been decelerating.

In the case of South Africa (and probably Lesotho), the average annual employment growth rate has been below the average annual labour force growth rate, as was the case in Swaziland between 1980 and 1990.[4] On the whole, formal sector employment in BLSN has not expanded fast enough to absorb all entrants into the labour force; however, the availability of wage employment in South Africa for BLNS citizens has provided a safety valve for employment pressures, but also a livelihood for many families. Remittances by migrant workers over the period 1987–89 averaged R96 million per annum in the case of Botswana, R160 million in the case of Lesotho and R40 million in the case of Swaziland.[5] All these figures suggest a significant

contribution to the development of the BLS. The range of manufactured products and utility sources available within SACU has always
been wide and readily accessible to all residents in the region. Even
though prices were not necessarily competitive with those in the rest
of the world, there have been serious shortages for a prolonged
period in all SACU member countries, suggesting the availability of
a wide enough range of products on which to exercise freedom of
economic choice (another dimension of development). That has not
been the case in the non-SACU countries of the region.

In assessing progress on a key SACU objective – namely, diversification and industrialization of the BLS economies – the evidence
suggests that there has been an unambiguous decline in the share of
primary production and an increase in the share of secondary
production (including manufacturing) for Lesotho and Swaziland.
For Botswana, the share of manufacturing has not increased substantially over the period in question though economic diversification
has certainly occurred.[6] Nevertheless, such diversification in BLS has
not reached the extent of that prevailing in the South African
economy, nor has it met the expectations prevailing at the time of
signing the CU agreement in 1969. The partial integration of labour
markets within SACU in the mining sector may have occurred at
some cost to the process of domestic diversification in BLSN and
resulted in a higher dependency of BLSN on South Africa than the
smaller countries would ideally like in order for their vulnerability to
disturbance in the South African economy to be reduced. Moreover,
the relatively small proportion of BLSN exports of non-agricultural
manufactures are indicative of the low extent of diversification that
has been achieved in these economies.

Exports from BLSN to South Africa have increased in the case of
Swaziland, but decreased in the case of Botswana in recent times.[7] To
the extent that most of the exports destined for South Africa are processed (such as molasses, cotton lint, wood products, paper products,
textiles, footwear and non-metallic mineral manufacturing), SACU
has probably encouraged (or at least not discouraged) some degree of
diversification in some of the BLSN countries.[8] However, the export
share for BLS has always been much less than import share, resulting
in a relatively large structural trade deficit for BLS *vis-à-vis* South
Africa suggesting, prima facie, that South African imports may have
inhibited domestic production in BLS so that these smaller markets

are dominated by South African manufacturers. As many observers have noted, the BLS markets have been quite important to the South African economy, especially in providing a protected market for its manufacturing exports.[9]

The share of CU receipts in total revenues has been declining for Botswana (mainly because of increasing government revenues from expanded domestic mining activities), but increasing for Swaziland, indicating slow progress in diversifying sources of revenue for Swaziland. Lesotho has always had an exceptionally high dependence on CU receipts. Slow growth in secondary and tertiary activities as alternative sources of government revenue reflects the lack of meaningful diversification in the BLSN economies already alluded to above. Thus, while there have been some structural shifts in the production of BLSN, there has not been as sufficient an increase in secondary production as the BLS economies required for their own development. The general view of BLSN governments and of independent experts is that the diversification of the BLSN economies, as envisaged in the third objective of SACU, has not been achieved to a perceptible extent. The SACU Agreement may have actually prevented that outcome from materializing as rapidly as it should have.

As for the objective of achieving an equitable distribution of benefits from trade among SACU members the benefits in question are the net result of trade creation and trade diversion effects. Each of these has both production and consumption aspects. In the context of trade creation, available evidence suggests that the benefits associated with production have accrued largely to South Africa, to the extent that net imports from South Africa were not produced in BLS originally, but were available from the rest of the world where prices were generally lower.[10] Thus, in so far as trade creation effects are concerned, equitable CU arrangements would require transfer of the benefits from trade to be made from South Africa to BLS. In the case of trade diversion, the sources of inputs for production and commodities for consumption from the perspective of BLSN are mainly in South Africa. The prices charged there are typically higher than those in the rest of the world as a result of the protective tariff wall and revenue-raising excise duties. Hence the net importer position of BLSN *vis-à-vis* South Africa suggests that BLSN residents have effectively subsidized South African industries for a long time. Again, equitable CU arrangements would indicate that compensatory transfers should be made from South Africa to BLSN for that reason as well.

Future prospects

Gavin Maasdorp has argued for an expanded and reorganized SACU as offering the most appropriate structure for future regional economic integration in southern Africa. In his words, SACU offers an 'advanced form of economic integration hardly matched elsewhere on the African continent'. 'It has proved', he argues, 'to be the most successful trade and monetary integrative project on the continent.' He concludes by asserting that, 'the SACU is the envy of the region and far in advance of anything COMESA and SADC have to offer'.[11] In reality, SACU is unlikely to provide the framework for greater regionalism for the simple reason that the ending of apartheid has not eradicated a general suspicion among countries of southern Africa of South Africa's imperial project. Even if we accept without qualification the proposition that SACU has been a success on the continent, the organization has historically been too associated with South Africa and dominated by decision-making in South Africa to provide a suitable model acceptable to the wider region. If this sounds speculative, then there is also a practical limitation. The noted success of SACU has been entirely due to the compensation mechanism. South Africa has in the past been willing to support SACU through a system of generous compensatory payments to the participant states so as to develop closer links with southern Africa. This not only lessened the threat of sanctions but also generated an export market for the sale of South Africa's manufactured goods. In 1981, Botswana, Lesotho and Swaziland (BLS) requested that the SACU Agreement be renegotiated. For various reasons talks about renegotiations are still continuing, and the parties have differing views about the appropriate emphasis and role of SACU.

One view from South Africa – at least from the Department of Trade and Industry (DTI) – is that South Africa is no longer receiving a sufficient share of the receipts because of an overly generous revenue-sharing formula that it can no longer afford. In 1969/70 BLS received 3.9 per cent of the common pool and South Africa 96.1 per cent. By 1990/91 the BLS share had increased to 17.1 per cent, with a further 8.3 per cent to the now independent Namibia, while Pretoria's share had fallen to 74.6 per cent.[12] With the end of apartheid and the sanctions threat removed, South Africa feels less inclined to subsidize such countries when confronted with the need to devote increasing amounts of capital to its neglected black population. More significantly, South Africa could certainly not afford to replicate for the whole region the generous compensatory payments at present received by the BLS states and Namibia. This view is further validated by the fact that the SACU Agreement did not allow for the possibility that the organization's tariffs might be reduced in terms of the WTO requirements for the liberalization of trade and also to make export from the region more competitive.

The Common Market for Eastern and Southern Africa

Established in 1993 the origins of COMESA can be traced back as far as the 1960s. At the first and second conferences of independent African states, held in Accra, Ghana in April 1958 and in Addis Ababa, Ethiopia in June 1960, economic problems to be faced by independent Africa were discussed. There was a consensus that the smallness and fragmentation of postcolonial African national markets would constitute a major obstacle to the diversification of economic activity away from a concentration on production of a narrow range of primary exports to the creation of modern and internationally competitive enterprises which would satisfy domestic needs and meet export requirements. It was, therefore, agreed that African countries which had gained political independence should promote economic cooperation among themselves. Two options were advocated for the implementation of the integration strategy in Africa: (a) the pan-African, all-embracing regional approach, which envisaged the immediate creation of a regional continental economic arrangement; and (b) the geographically narrower approach that would have its roots at the subregional levels and build on subregional cooperation arrangements to achieve geographically wider forms of cooperation arrangements.[13]

For geostrategic reasons, the majority of the countries favoured the narrower subregional approach. Based on this, the United Nations Economic Commission for Africa (ECA) proposed the division of the continent into four subregions: Eastern and Southern, Central, West and North Africa. The OAU Conference of Heads of State and Government adopted the Commission's proposals. All independent African states were enjoined to take, during the 1980s, all necessary steps to strengthen existing subregional economic cooperative groupings and, as necessary, establish new ones so as to cover the whole continent subregion by subregion and promote coordination and harmonization among the groupings for the gradual establishment of an African Economic Community by the end of the century.

In April 1980 Heads of State and Government of the OAU, together with representatives of the Economic Commission for Africa (ECA), met in Lagos – the capital of Nigeria – to discuss initiatives for promoting economic development and stability in Africa. This Lagos meeting led in 1981 to the creation of the Preferential Trade Area for Eastern and Southern Africa (PTA). PTA was based on customs union theory with a great emphasis on the elimination of intra-area barriers and the equalization of tariffs on import from non-member states. Specifically, the PTA aimed to promote:[14]

- evolution within the PTA area of complementary transport and communication policies and systems, and measures to expand the existing transport and communications links among countries in the PTA to establish new ones so as to facilitate cross-border movement of goods, capital, labour and services;
- specializations and complementarity within the PTA in the productive sectors (within and across sectors and country borders) of agriculture and industry, along with the development of research and training facilities to improve enterprise and efficiency and product quality;
- higher standards of living within the PTA by fostering closer relations among its member states.

These objectives were not realized because of the economic strategies adopted within PTA member countries to accelerate their individual development. Until the late 1980s and early 1990s most PTA countries followed an economic strategy which involved the state in all aspects of production, distribution and marketing, thus denying the private sector an economic role to play, except as shopkeepers, and promoting import substitution and subsidized consumption. The theory was that successful emerging industries could be identified by the state and nurtured through a system of subsidies, grants and protection from foreign competition behind a high tariff wall, and that these industries could then grow to a size from which they could compete against foreign firms. This did not actually happen as the domestic markets were too small in terms of purchasing power for industries to realize economies of scale; lack of competition resulted in poor quality goods being produced; foreign direct investment was actively discouraged, resulting in insufficient levels of investment taking place in both capital and labour and in low levels of technology transfer; and there was a lack of complementarity between domestic industries.

Initially, import substitution programmes were financed from domestic earnings such as revenues realized from the sale of primary agricultural commodities and minerals. As levels of revenue from these sources declined, owing to declining terms of trade and reduced efficiencies in production systems, these countries started borrowing on western capital markets, and from the World Bank and IMF, to maintain previous levels of consumption. As many of the countries concerned were at this stage considered to be middle-income countries, they borrowed at commercial rates. The borrowed money was usually not used to improve production so real levels of GDP continued to decline while expenditure levels, which had by then risen significantly as a result of higher debt servicing payments, continued to increase.

Governments of PTA countries faced these economic crises by continuing to borrow on international markets; by placing heavy restrictions on foreign currency transactions to try to reduce capital flight; by pegging the value of the local currency against freely convertible foreign currencies artificially high to reduce costs of essential imports (such as fuel which in itself caused crises in the early 1970s); by using revenues from parastatal industries to finance the public sector recurrent budget, leaving little revenue for reinvestment in these strategic industries which resulted in further declines in production; by reducing the import bill by restricting by statute items which could be imported; and by heavily subsidizing all aspects of domestic agricultural production to promote self-sufficiency in food production, which only served to make agriculture sectors even more inefficient than they already were.

In an attempt to reverse the declining fortunes of its member states, the PTA reinvented itself in 1993 into the Common Market for Eastern and Southern Africa (COMESA). The treaty outlined the following as the aims and objectives of the new organization:

- to attain sustainable growth and development of the member states by promoting a more balanced and harmonious development of its production and marketing structures;
- to promote joint development in all fields of economic activity and the joint adoption of macro-economic policies and programmes to raise the standard of living of its people and to foster closer relations among its member states;
- to cooperate in the creation of an environment for foreign, cross-border and domestic investment including the joint promotion of research and adoption of science and technology for development;
- to cooperate in the promotion of peace, security and stability among member states in order to enhance economic development in the region;
- to cooperate in strengthening the relations between the Common Market and the rest of the world and the adoption of a common position in international fora; and
- to contribute towards the establishment, progress and realization of the objectives of the African Economic Community.

As envisaged by the Lagos Plan and the more recent Abuja Declaration, issues related to trade liberalization, facilitation, promotion and financing were supposed to be resolved in a major effort to establish a Common Market of Eastern and Southern African States by 2000. There is no evidence to suggest that COMESA has been particularly successful at achieving any of its original objectives. Where trade liberalization is concerned the main issue of importance is tariff barriers to trade. With regard to this the agreed target for their removal was to reduce them by 10 per cent every two years between 1 October 1988 and 1 October 1996 with a review in 1996 to determine how the remaining 50 per cent should be eliminated by 2000.[14] It was suggested that if the Lagos Plan of Action were to be used as a guiding principle, then 2000 could be improved to 1998 and the remaining 30 per cent in the year 2000.[15] Progress on the implementation of these tariff reductions has been very slow.[16]

Reporting on progress in March 2000, only Mauritius, Uganda and Zimbabwe have complied with the dates set by the Council of Ministers. Burundi, Ethiopia, Kenya, Malawi, Mozambique, Rwanda, Somalia, Sudan and Zambia had not yet published the second tariff reduction.[17] Malawi and Burundi maintain that publication of further reductions is meaningless as other member states are reluctant to give licences for goods to be imported from their countries.[18] Not surprisingly, the final reduction has not been met by member states; most of them are still to implement the second tariff reduction.

Problems associated with timetable compliance notwithstanding, member states seem to also have difficulties in ratifying COMESA protocols. At the end of 1999 there were 27 legal instructions pending ratification by member states; today there are over 33. Angola, Djibouti, Mozambique, Somalia and Sudan have not ratified any of the 23 legal instructions. Even the conventions which member states agreed to accede to have not yet formally been approved by several members. These include, for example, the Convention on the Recognition and Enforcement of Foreign Arbitral Award (New York, 1958). Countries that have acceded to this Convention are Djibouti, Kenya, Lesotho, Rwanda, Swaziland, Tanzania, Uganda, Zambia and Zimbabwe, but only nine countries out of 18 have complied with the COMESA agreement to accede to this convention. It is the same story with the Convention on the Simplification and Harmonization of Customs Procedures (Kyoto Convention, 1973). There are 21 member states party to this convention but Kenya, Lesotho, Rwanda, Tanzania, Uganda, Zambia and Zimbabwe are the only seven out of the 21 to have implemented this COMESA agreement.

COMESA has also agreed that member states should incorporate the provisions of the organization's treaty into their domestic laws.[19] Only seven countries have complied with this agreement, i.e. Burundi, Ethiopia, Kenya, Malawi, Rwanda, Sudan and Zimbabwe. It is evident that existing incentives and mechanisms for conforming with COMESA agreements are insufficiently strong to induce member

Table 4.1   Total intra-COMESA trade (US$ m)

	1980	*1985*	*1988*	*1990*	*1992*	*1993*	*1994*
Intra-COMESA trade	1254.7	834.22	1160.76	1174.2	1222.56	1499.84	1707.28
Intra-COMESA export	627.35	486.68	587.10	579.01	611.28	749.92	853.64
Intra-COMESA import	627.35	417.11	580.38	879.01	611.28	749.92	853.64

Source: Various COMESA trade statistics.

Table 4.2   COMESA in figures

Country	Total exports 1996 (US$ m)	Total imports 1996 (US$ m)	Intra-COMESA exports 1996 (US$ m)	Intra-COMESA imports 1996 (US$ m)
Angola	2864	1299	2	4
Burundi	175	253	13	29
Comoros	55	114	0	9
Ethiopia & Eritrea	302	1125	0	21
Kenya	1658	2739	374	43
Lesotho	83	65	0	5
Madagascar	531	600	13	19
Malawi	352	450	31	52
Mauritius	1254	1999	31	32
Mozambique	222	1200	5	57
Namibia	612	289	5	6
Rwanda	72	310	1	60
Sudan	515	1320	0	30
Swaziland	290	80	14	9
Tanzania	500	1530	61	132
Uganda	370	580	8	120
Zaire	1200	1100	5	52
Zambia	760	620	72	46
Zimbabwe	1800	2120	213	47

Source: Various UNDP and COMESA Reports.

states to comply within a reasonable period. Delays in implementing these agreements have consequences for trade, for the credibility of COMESA and for the commitment of its members to achieving the progressive reduction of intra-regional trade barriers.

With the exception of Lesotho and Swaziland (which as members of SACU have obtained temporary exemptions) all other member states have complied with the first 10 per cent tariff reduction. However, there has been no discernible impact by way of increased trade among COMESA countries as a result – see Table 4.1. As is evident from Table 4.1 intra-COMESA trade increased from US$1254.7 million in 1980 to US$1707.28 in 1994. In real terms, this increase is very marginal and represents between 4.6 per cent to 5.4 per cent of the total trade of member states – see Table 4.2.[20]

In terms of export totals within COMESA, there was a marginal increase from US$627.35 million in 1980 to US$853.64 million in

1994.[21] In 1984 Kenya exported US$340 million to other COMESA countries; by 1994 this figure had dropped to US$218 million. Kenya was the largest exporter to other COMESA countries in both 1980 and 1989.[22] Tanzania exported US$56 million to COMESA in 1980 but by 1993 its export had declined to only US$9.4 million. In 1985 it was the second largest exporter but by 1994 it had dropped to ninth position. Mozambique was the third biggest exporter to COMESA in 1980 with US$52 million.[23] Zambia and Zimbabwe seem to have increased their exports to COMESA. In 1980, Zambia exported US$36 million and this increased steadily to US$69 million in 1994. Similarly, Zimbabwe exported US$29 million to COMESA in 1984 and this increased steadily to US$153 million in 1994; it is now the second largest exporter to COMESA.[24]

Intra-COMESA import figures show a similar trend – see Table 4.3. In 1985 Uganda was the highest importer from other COMESA countries with US$198 million; in 1996 this figure dropped to US$135 million. Kenya was the second biggest importer at US$65 million in 1985 but by 1996 this figure dropped to only US$43 million.[25] Burundi imported US$32.61 million in 1985, but that declined to US$29 million in 1996. Countries like Zambia, Zimbabwe, Mozambique and Rwanda increased their imports from COMESA: Zambia increased its imports from US$36 million in 1985 to US$60 million in 1996; Zimbabwe from US$21 million to US$47 million; Mozambique from US$22 million to US$82 million; and Rwanda from US$40 million to US$42 million in the same period.

There are three explanations for this decline in intra-COMESA trade over the decade. First, there was a general decline in external

Table 4.3 Intra-COMESA imports from selected countries 1980–96 (US$ m)

	1980	*1985*	*1988*	*1990*	*1992*	*1994*	*1996*
Comoros	11.53	3.58	3.00	4.00	7.00	7.4	8.3
Burundi	34.61	32.61	25.00	26.00	26.00	25	29
Kenya	121	65.71	46.99	39.90	72.11	39.00	43.00
Tanzania	22.01	27.00	39.00	41.00	53.00	104.00	135.00
Uganda	195	86.78	95.00	198.00	130.00	118.00	135.00
Zimbabwe	35.12	21.90	46.00	129.00	62.00	43.00	47.00

Source: Various COMESA trade statistics.

trade for the countries involved. As their economies have contracted and foreign exchange shortages have become particularly acute, their ability to trade has also declined – hence the low level of activity within COMESA. Second, COMESA members have preferred trading with non-members partly because of the hard currency earning potential from exports and the absence of capacity in the region to produce the full range of capital, intermediate and consumer manufactures that these countries import. Third, imports of COMESA members have become increasingly donor-financed during the 1980s while import trade has shifted to donors as source countries because of full or partial aid-typing whereas the bulk of COMESA exports remain primary products exported to hard currency areas.

For the COMESA countries as a whole, exports increased from US$8.46 billion in 1980 to US$15 billion in 1999.[26] Six countries experienced a decline in exports (Uganda, Tanzania, Swaziland, Mozambique, Malawi and Kenya); the remaining COMESA members (and especially Mauritius) increased their exports significantly between 1990 and 1999.[27] Total imports of COMESA member countries from the rest of the world including export increased from US$10.7 billion to US$13 billion over the same period. In 1990 Kenya was the biggest exporter with US$2326 million. There was a decline in imports between 1994 and 1997 but imports started to rise during 1998 and 1999.[28] In 1999 they stood at US$2400 million. The second biggest exporter was Sudan at US$1303 million in 1998. Imports from Angola remained more or less constant over the period. Zimbabwe's and Zambia's imports rose from US$219 million and US$747 million in 1989 to US$1900 million and US$792 million in 1999 respectively.[29]

The relative share of intra-COMESA trade to the overall trade of members is small – see Table 4.2. As a percentage of total exports between 1980 and 1996, Burundi exported 42 per cent to COMESA with this share remaining constant between 1980 and 1996. Kenya's exports to COMESA fell from 24.5 per cent to 19 per cent. Mozambique's fell from 11 per cent to only 1 per cent, and Ethiopia's from 14.4 per cent to 5 per cent. Mauritian exports to COMESA were insignificant. Tanzania's exports to COMESA declined from 10 per cent to 3 per cent, while Rwanda increased its exports to COMESA from 9 per cent to 20 per cent. A similar trend was observed in the case of Zambia (from 2.8 per cent to 7.5 per cent), Zimbabwe (from 5 per cent to 11 per cent) and Swaziland (from 1 per cent to 7 per cent).[30]

As a share of total imports in 1980 and 1996 Djibouti's imports from COMESA declined from 27 per cent to only 8 per cent; Burundi's from 22 per cent to 16 per cent; those of Comoros from 17 per cent to 6 per cent; Kenya's from 3 per cent to 1.6 per cent; Rwanda's from 19 per cent to 11 per cent; Somalia's from 12 per cent to 7 per cent; Swaziland's from 9 per cent to 3 per cent; Uganda's from 46 per cent to 24 per cent; and Zimbabwe's from 16 per cent to 5 per cent in the same ten-year period. Most members of COMESA have increased their imports from non-members. Even countries which exported a significant fraction of their total exports to COMESA such as Rwanda, Zimbabwe, Swaziland and Djibouti have imported mainly from elsewhere. In large part this is because of the larger role played by bilateral grant aid flows in financing imports in most COMESA countries, and because apart from Kenya and Zimbabwe there are no COMESA countries which produce the type of imports which most COMESA members need.

Prospects for greater regionalism

Progress in pursuit of the goal of converting COMESA into a common market has so far been uneven. There are several obstacles that lie in the way of achieving this objective. First, the lack of sanctions or incentives in fulfilling the requirements of tariff reduction may be partly responsible for the absence of urgency with which tariff reduction has been implemented so far. Moreover, it is clear that tariff reduction alone is unlikely to have a significant impact on intra-COMESA trade expansion. Protective import substitution strategies adopted by most member states since independence have also resulted in a host of regulations restricting trade such as licensing, administrative foreign exchange allocation, special tax for acquiring foreign exchange, advance import deposits, etc. Secondly, intra-COMESA trade needs to be promoted through the simplification and streamlining of the many different regulations and procedures related to customs, transit documents and customs bond guarantees. The unavailability of sufficient trade financing is also a major barrier in COMESA countries. In that connection the efforts of COMESA to mobilize and encourage the efforts of commercial banks are well directed and need to be strengthened. However, the role and value of the COMESA bank has not been fully demonstrated and the need for its continued existence requires careful reconsideration. Though the

COMESA bank has undertaken many useful trade financing initiatives these can easily be folded into an expanded COMESA clearing house. On the development financing front it is clear what role the COMESA bank can play.

The creation of a common market (in the commonly understood sense of that term) by the year 2000 was unlikely to be achieved. Indeed it is doubtful that, with the lack of sanctions/incentives applicable to member states for not complying with the timetable for tariff reduction, even that limited objective can be achieved by the end of 2005. Harmonization of the various trade documents procedures, transit documents and customs bond guarantees issues, will take at least the next 10–15 years to complete, and a similar period will need to elapse before COMESA member states develop sufficient confidence in institutions such as the clearing house to utilize it fully. Wars and conflicts in COMESA have devastated transport networks, communications and other basic infrastructure for trade in countries like Angola, Ethiopia, Sudan, Somalia and Mozambique. It will take at least another 10–15 years before their infrastructures are restored to the level they were at in 1970. For a common market to function its members need to be at least at peace. Several regional security matters still need to be resolved in the COMESA area, and so building institutions for COMESA trade without the resolution of regional security issues may border on wishful thinking. Moreover, it will take another decade or two before COMESA members are in a position to harmonize their fiscal and monetary regimes to a level where their effective integration becomes a viable possibility. For all of these reasons, a common market by the year 2000 remains a pipe dream. COMESA members are far too diverse and as a group do not yet have the capability or the commitment at the national level to make integration a workable reality in the foreseeable future.

The Southern African Development Community

In 1992 the Southern African Development Coordination Conference (SADCC) became the Southern African Development Community (SADC). Unlike its antecedent, SADC is based on a legally binding treaty ratified by all member states. Its principle objectives include following economic goals:

- to achieve development and economic growth, alleviate poverty, enhance the standard and quality of life of the peoples of southern Africa, and support the socially disadvantaged through regional integration;
- to promote and maximize productive employment and utilization of resources of the region; and
- to achieve sustainable utilization of natural resources and effective protection of the environment.

To achieve these objectives, SADC proposed to:

- harmonize political and socio-economic policies and plans of member states;
- mobilize the peoples of the region and their institutions to take initiatives to develop economic, social and cultural ties across the region, and to participate fully in the implementation of the programmes and operations of SADC and its institutions;
- develop policies aimed at the progressive elimination of obstacles to free movement of capital and labour, goods and services and of the peoples of the region generally among member states;
- promote the development of human resources;
- promote the development, transfer and mastery of technology;
- improve economic management and performance through regional cooperation.

Given that in practice anti-South African sentiment rather than economic common interests bound the SADCC together, it was hardly surprising that initially its metamorphosis into SADC was not indicative of a major change in policy for the international community. Indeed, for the wider international community, the only significant departure in principle was a new preference for a dirigiste over a laissez-faire approach: regional integration was to be driven by a more regimented, interventionist and centrally directed policy, although the institutional structures and policy content of this reorientation were not specified. At a critical reading it appears that SADC has to be understood within the context of the Lomé IV Convention. That is, it appears that changes in Europe's view of the role of the SADCC within the convention provided the catalyst for the organization's reorientation. Title XII of Lomé IV is specifically devoted to regional cooperation, and as stated in Article 150:

> The Community shall support the ACP state efforts through regional co-operation to promote long-term collective and self-reliant, self-sustained and integrated social, cultural and economic development and greater regional self-sufficiency. Community support shall be given within the framework of the major regional co-operation and integration objectives which the ACP states have set or will set for themselves at regional, inter-regional and inter-national level.

In contrast to earlier Lomé Conventions, greater emphasis was placed upon economic integration and functional cooperation, with approximately one-tenth of the entire budget (1250 million ecu) allocated for such regional initiatives globally during the period 1990–95. The member states of SADC were further advantaged by three special provisions for ACP countries that were 'least developed' and land-locked. Prior to Lomé IV, SADC's programme of action had been the exclusive avenue for EU funding. However, from 1990 onwards the 121 million ecu allocated specifically for southern Africa were also available for preferential trade area (PTA) projects which traditionally were more dedicated to the principle of free trade and establishing a common market.[31] In addition, the threat of increased and internationally legitimate competition (as opposed to illegitimate economic domination) from South Africa sounded the death knell for the *raison d'être* of the SADCC.

Achievements and limitations

Despite severe economic problems caused by recession in the world economy, lengthy periods of drought and the destabilization that plagued the region in the 1980s, many would concur that the SADCC had some positive results.[32] In the words of Morna, the SADCC arrangements can be considered as 'one of Africa's few successful attempts at regional co-operation'.[33] Morna concludes that 'to a large extent, this bears testimony to the political will and determination that inspire the countries that are its members, despite their continuing economic vulnerability.' Certainly, despite the broader structural limitations faced by SADC countries, their endeavours were partly

Table 4.4 SADC projects financing status by (selected) sector ($ million), 1990–98

Sector	No. of projects	Total amount	Foreign amount %	Local amount %	Secured amount %	Gap amount %
Energy	92	679.90	651.22 97.07	19.68 2.93	182.29 27.17	488.61 72.83
Industry and trade	15	23.72	23.30 98.23	0.42 1.77	5.58 23.95	17.65 74.41
Mining	43	81.81	77.86 95.17	3.95 4.83	39.08 47.77	42.73 52.23
Manpower development	33	22.50	22.23 98.80	0.27 1.20	13.83 61.47	8.67 38.53
Tourism	8	81.81	10.27 97.90	0.22 2.10	2.56 24.40	7.93 75.60
Transportation and communications	218	6078.60	5349.70 88.01	728.90 11.99	2423.60 39.87	3296.90 54.25
Agricultural research	17	259.23	246.40 95.05	12.83 4.95	74.85 28.87	229.69 63.02
Fisheries and wildlife	56	364.48	352.10 96.60	12.38 3.40	123.84 33.98	229.69 63.02
Soil and water conservation	13	65.13	54.86 84.23	10.27 15.77	22.43 34.44	42.70 65.56
Food security	36	186.58	148.89 79.80	37.69 20.20	62.58 33.54	122.53 65.67
Livestock and disease cont.	15	111.67	65.19 58.38	46.48	76.08 68.13	35.59 31.87
Grand total	*546*	*7875.11*	*7002.02* *88.91*	*873.09* *11.09*	*3026.82* *38.44*	*4477.30* *56.85*

Source: SADC Reports 1989–95.

successful in attaining some of the goals established in the Lusaka Declaration. Two in particular should be stressed, namely the mobilization of resources to implement national, inter-state and regional policies, and concerted action to guarantee international cooperation in the context of a strategy for economic liberation.

At the end of the 1980s SADC developed 571 projects for funding and secured US$2675 million in financing from a number of donors. The major thrust of SADC's activities was the rehabilitation and development of the physical infrastructure of the region, particularly in transportation and communication. Of particular importance is the positive evolution in the upgrading and development of the corridors and regional airports (cases in point are Dar es Salaam, Gaborone, Kilimanjaro, Lilongwe, Maseru and Matsapa), as well as in carrying out the energy programmes. By early 1991, Mozambique's Beira corridor port was handling about two million tons of cargo annually. After current rehabilitation work is completed, the capacity of the port is expected to rise to five million tons annually.[34] Sixty per cent of transit traffic from the six landlocked states was moving through SADC ports in 1991, as compared with 20 per cent in 1980.[35] SADC member states are now connected directly by satellite telecommunications, which were previously routed through South Africa. Furthermore, all SADC capitals are now linked directly by air (see Table 4.5).

In comparison to other regional organizations in Africa, SADC members have also enjoyed some success in obtaining aid from international development institutions like the World Bank, as well as various government aid agencies. The World Bank 1992 world debt report estimated that the flow of aid per capita to the region during the 1980s was three times the average for the Third World.

Table 4.5 Number of civil flight services per week between the SADCC member states

Year:	*1985*	*1986*	*1987*	*1988*	*1989*
No. of services	133	136	198	224	258
% increase		2%	46%	13%	15%

Source: SADCC (1989) *Annual Progress Report 1988–1989*. Gaborone, p. 49.

Despite the low share of Third World population (2 per cent) and Third World GDP (1 per cent), the region received more than 7 per cent of total development assistance. Endorsing this position, in 1988 the World Bank's Vice-President for Africa, Edward Jaycox, described SADC as a 'functional example of how regional cooperation in Africa might work'.[36]

On closer inspection, the SADC success is misleading. On balance, only the BLSN countries experienced any growth in per capita incomes between 1980 and 1994. The others experienced prolonged economic recessions of varying severity with declining per capita income through the 1980s and earlier 1990s. Mozambique, Namibia and Zambia experienced the most spectacular decline, while Zimbabwe, Malawi and Tanzania declined less severely. In 1995 the economic performance of SADC members showed a modest improvement – except for Zambia whose GDP continued to decline, but despite the turnaround only Botswana, Lesotho, Malawi and Swaziland has positive growth in per capita incomes.[37] Aggregate indicators of their economic performance do not suggest that, for the period of its existence, SADC had any significant impact on improving the economic circumstances of its member states. The counterfactual argument that without SADC the economic circumstances of its members might have been even worse is, of course, difficult to make with any conviction. Obviously SADC cannot be faulted for the failure of national economic policies or for adverse external economic circumstances. The prolonged economic distress of most of its members undoubtedly impairs SADC's own effectiveness and limits its scope for operation. A decade of adjustment pressures which have led to public expenditure and investment cutbacks with a focus on policy reform throughout the region almost certainly operated to the detriment of project investment in most SADC member states thus undercutting SADC's operating ground.

In addition, little progress has been made with respect to the reduction of dependency on South Africa. This is graphically illustrated with reference to trade. Regional cooperation, as measured by intra-SADC trade, was estimated to be around 5 per cent of the members' total external trade, with Zimbabwe accounting for over 80 per cent of this figure by the end of the 1980s.[38] In 1995 trade flows between South Africa and the SADC countries exceeded intra-SADC transactions by 4 : 1. While there is some debate about the magnitude of trade between South Africa and SADC, the strategic importance of South Africa is clearly evident. It is estimated that in 1990 SADC members sent 9 per cent of their total exports to South Africa, whereas 30 per cent of their imports were sourced in the Republic. SADC members in SACU, the BLS countries and Namibia, make up a large proportion of this percentage. Manufactured goods continue to constitute the bulk (up to 95 per cent) of imports in the SADC countries, except in Zimbabwe. Maasdorp estimates that SADC's exports of merchandise and services to SADC destinations more than doubled between 1984 and 1987, underlining the importance of the SADC market for South Africa's manufacturing industry. The constraints acting against any increase in regional trade are a lack of tradable goods and services, a similarity, if not uniformity, of products and serious payment and foreign exchange problems in most SADC member states.

South Africa's accession into SADC in 1994 has had several important implications for the functioning of the organization. These include, first, growing competition between post-apartheid South Africa and Zimbabwe – the only other industrialized economy in the region; second, the allocation of the strategic financial and investment sector within SADC to South Africa; third, the recent accession of Mauritius, the Democratic Republic of the Congo and Seychelles raises the broader question as to the future relationship between SADC and the 23-member COMESA.

Conclusion

The question arises of choosing the optimal route to arriving at a single institutional framework within which southern African states can productively cooperate without excessive disruption of present arrangements and without compromising the gains that have already been derived from them. There are, of course, several permutations of how a process of institutional modification and eventual merger might occur within and across the three separate organizational frames. To help discern between the possible alternatives, a questionnaire was undertaken to ascertain the business community's view of the existing organizations.[39] Firms were asked to state their preference for possible alternative future courses for the SADC, SACU and

Table 4.6   Views of firms on future regional groupings (%)

	Yes	*No*	*Uncertain*
SACU to become a common market	54.9	25.6	19.5
SACU/SADC merger	71.5	7.9	20.6
PTA/SADC merger	27.8	70.7	13.5

COMESA (see Table 4.6). The response rates were sufficiently good in Botswana, Zimbabwe and South Africa (around 87 per cent), while Lesotho and Namibia were satisfactory (around 61 per cent). For Malawi and Swaziland, the response rate was rather small (around 40 per cent). Altogether, 361 firms in the region responded to the questionnaires.

In the first pairing, the alternatives were for SACU to remain as it is or for it to become a common market (the difference was explained in the questionnaires). A majority (54.9 per cent) favoured the idea of a common market; 25.6 per cent wanted no change, and the rest were uncertain. Uncertainty was greatest in Lesotho, while firms in Swaziland were significantly more in favour of a common market than those in the other three countries. This question was also included in the Malawi survey out of interest: 63.3 per cent favoured SACU becoming a common market and the balance were uncertain. In the second pairing, firms were asked to choose between SACU and SADC remaining as they are or merging into a single trading area, i.e. free trade area or customs union (the meaning of which was explained in the questionnaires). In SACU countries 70.1 per cent were in favour of merger and 10 per cent wanted the status quo to remain. Firms in Botswana were slightly better disposed (77.7 per cent) to a merger, and firms in Lesotho were more uncertain (31.6 per cent). This question was also included in the Zimbabwe questionnaires: 74.2 per cent favoured a merger and 3.4 per cent the status quo. For the six countries together, 71.5 per cent favoured a merger. The third pairing requested firms to choose between SADC and COMESA remaining as they are or merging. Over 70 per cent of the responses were against a merger and most indicated a preference for SADC to remain independent of COMESA.

These results seem to indicate that the SACU and SADC arrangements were strongly favoured by the private sector in member countries. In general, firms were less certain with regard to membership of COMESA. Firms in Lesotho, Swaziland and Namibia were overwhelmingly in favour of SACU membership given a choice between SACU and COMESA. This is not surprising given their close links to the South African economy. Equally, firms in Zimbabwe and Malawi were also strongly in favour of SACU membership for their country. About two-thirds of firms in member countries, and 60 per cent of those in the surveyed countries, favoured SADC membership. Large percentages were uncertain. A slightly lower percentage of firms were in favour of COMESA. Thus the SADC appears to enjoy more support among regional firms than COMESA. Some 55 per cent of firms in SACU favoured it becoming a common market. The majority of firms in Malawi favoured SACU becoming a common market. Since the majority also favoured membership for Malawi, it appears to indicate that they would favour a deep form of integration between their country and SACU. The majority of firms favoured a merger between SADC and SACU into a single trading area.

5
Rethinking Regional Security in Southern Africa

It is quite remarkable that in spite of apartheid southern African states have developed an increasingly active and dense network of private as well as public ties that bind them together in an interdependent economic, political and cultural system. The rising volume of trade flows, cross-border investments, interlocking financial deals, diplomatic consultations, cultural exchanges and tourism manifests these ties. At the same time, government officials, business leaders and academic scholars have been gathering with increasing frequency in regional capitals to discuss problems of regional concern and to search for institutional frameworks for joint action. The immediate aims of this chapter are twofold: to explore security from a human perspective; and to illustrate this perspective by drawing upon case material from southern Africa. The underlying objective is to help generate an alternative debate and understanding of security and its implications for state survival in the region.

Traditional security

During the Cold War, the concept of security was taken to mean national political and military security. Not surprisingly the study of security came to focus on nation-states as both agents and objects of the most significant occurrence in world politics. Specifically, the concept became virtually synonymous with 'defence'. Crucial here were two underlying assumptions: first, that threat to a state's security principally arose from outside its borders; and second, that these threats were primarily, if not exclusively, military in nature and usually required military response if the security of the target state was to be preserved.[1] Accordingly, security came to focus on war, the ability to fight wars and the external threats to the state which might give rise to them. For the analyst, the referent object of security became the state. In this world, security came from being a citizen, and insecurity from citizens of other states. The state was thus depicted as the protector of its citizens from the hostile intentions of other states. These threats from other states were seen as 'directed toward individuals *qua* citizens (that is, toward their states), and the study of security accordingly strives to mitigate these threats through concerted action by the representatives of the citizenry – the state leaders'.[2] Societal security in this context was underplayed, or examined specifically in the context of the legitimacy of the governing structure of any particular state. Thus such issues as inter-state and intra-state migration, environmental protection, food and water security and job security, to name but a few, were either not dealt with or dismissed as domestic political matters. The odious nature of realism in the context of the Cold War, it appears, was sufficient to discourage scholars and commentators from investigating the critical nature of security.

Since the end of the Cold War the concept of security has been redefined (Mathews, 1989; Poku and Graham, 1998; Graham and Poku, 1999; Thomas and Wilkin, 1998; Baldwin, 1997), reconceptualized (Håkan, 1992), reshaped (Krause and Williams, 1996), retheorized (Wyn Jones, 1989; Booth, 1991), re-examined (Buzan, 1995) and revisioned (Lipschutz, 1995). The resulting conceptual muddle has allowed some to claim not so much a redefinition as a de-definition of security (Weaver, 1995).[3]

In spite of this attention, however, it is still rare to find the security interests of states separated, even conceptually, from those of the people under them, less still the international security of persons and groups of people, rather than states, made the focus of attention. In the majority of literature on International Relations, state policies always appear both well-defined and comprehensive enough to exclude nothing that mattered to the 'national interest'. In this literature, the state remains the censorious referent of security and the concept becomes synonymous with the defence of the 'national interest'. Security in this context is conceived internally as the repression of dissidence while externally it involves espionage and massive arms proliferation, in particular the development of ever more sophisticated weapons of mass destruction. Accordingly, the study of security has come to focus on war, the ability to fight wars and the external threats to the state which might give rise to them.

At a deeper level, this conception of security was indebted to the ontological insights of the dominant paradigm of the day – Realism.[4] Following the writings of Machiavelli and Hobbes, realism is grounded in a pessimistic conception of human nature. In general, human beings are perceived to have a problematic nature: they are uninformed, passionate, undisciplined and even violent. Moreover, they lack the intelligence to perform rational cost–benefit calculations and are incapable of discarding their own best interest, and even if they do, they lack the willpower to act in accordance with those interests. This view of man is tied to a specific image of the state. Because man cannot find fulfilment and salvation within himself he must find it outside himself – in the collectivity, in the state.[5] The state compensates for the deficiencies of man: where man is passionate, the state is rational; where man is weak, the state is strong – it possesses reason and will, there is a *raison d'état* and a *volonté d'état*. States have intelligence and will to survive; they are rational actors, entailing a state-centred perception of world politics.[6] Yet states are not entirely rational. They have a dualistic nature – there is a certain potential to unreason in each state. They may at times lose their will to exist or they may endanger the existence of other states by pursuing a 'revisionist' policy.

According to this realist view, the state needs an elite because it must survive in a hostile environment, at home and abroad. At home it confronts the irrational masses of citizens – abroad, a host of hostile powers. The supreme goal is to survive in this two-sided state of war, and to succeed, the state is highly centralized and hierarchical.[7] It is a tight collectivity in which individuals are means serving a higher end, subordinate parts of a whole with well-defined functions and roles. Their values are not individualistic, they do not emphasize independence, self-determination, self-discipline, voluntariness and equality. Within this kind of state the emphasis is on dependence, subordination, involuntariness and inequality in pursuit of the 'national interest'.

Externally, the state has to be strong because it confronts others of a similar kind – hence the anarchical nature of the international system. The result, according to Waltz (1979), is a decentralized system where conflict is endemic and security is managed by self-help. Each state has to provide for its own security. Each state is forced to arm. Economic considerations are subordinate to military considerations because, although states engage in international trade, this engagement is fragile because states worry about the relative gains accruing from international exchange, gains that directly affect their relative position of strength. In this context, cooperation is temporary because states only cooperate for purely egotistical reasons – concerned with counterbalancing a potential hegemon. As a result, international trade and interdependence must not be valued too highly. The impact of the 'forces of modernity', of science, technology, communication and commerce, is ambivalent: they can strengthen or weaken a country. This is a world of no permanent friendship or enmities but of constantly changing alliances dictated by no other sentiment (such as religion, ideology or dynastic bonds) than the 'reason of state'.

Statesmen are not expected actively to seek conflict but they must regard war as a rational instrument and have to be willing to use it when necessary.[8] At times, war can be avoided because the mere threat of war (deterrence) will suffice, but it is important to prepare for the worst case. To that end, it is vital to be in possession of a broad range of military instruments to handle any situation and to control any crisis. Insufficient armament and particularly disarmament leads to a power vacuum and to unstable situations inviting aggression and causing war.[9] Stability in the international system is more likely when all states are sufficiently secure and armed. Perpetual peace is impossible – at best there can be stability through the adroit management of alliances that counterbalance potential hegemons.

Accordingly, security came to focus on war, the ability to fight wars and the external threats to the state which might give rise to them.[10] Societal security in this context is underplayed, or examined specifically in the context of the legitimacy of the governing structure of any particular state. Thus, such issues as interstate and intrastate migration, environmental protection, food and water security, job security, to name but a few, were either not dealt with or dismissed as domestic political matters. The odious nature of realism in the context of the Cold War, it appears, was sufficient to discourage scholars and commentators from investigating the critical nature of human security.

Rethinking security

The transition out of the cold war purview demands that we go back to the drawing board and determine whether the philosophical ontology from which much of the realist arguments are built is still intact. Paradigms are not, as Gadamer puts it, 'rendered anonymous'.[11] That is, they are not constructed in a vacuum. On the contrary, they are always constructed by individuals with a definite view from a particular background and at a certain time in history. In this sense, 'theory is', indeed, 'always for someone and for some purpose'.[12] Hence, all theories have a perspective which derives from historical time and geographic space. Yet to agree with the assertion that 'there is no appropriate scale available with which to weigh the merits of alternative paradigms' is to strike an attitude.[13] Indeed, this attitude would be even greater if we are led to believe that to favour one paradigm rather than another is simply a preference which cannot be 'rationalised by any non-circular argument'.[14] If theories are, indeed, 'incommensurable' then how can one critically assess the merits of a theory? Similarly, if theories 'cannot be rationalised by any non-circular argument', then what is the purpose of applying intellectual rigour to that area of academic study? None, certainly, if one accepts or rejects theories purely on the basis of 'personal preference'. At one level, Barnes is right to highlight the difficult nature of paradigmic evaluation, but wrong to posit such a fatalistic note to the process.

In truth, there are criteria we can apply which will identify at least the strength and weaknesses of a paradigm, if not its overall merit. These criteria derive from the philosophical basis of understanding international relations and, like most western social sciences, employ a particular though widely accepted notion of epistemology. The epistemology of international relations here provides the meta-theory which enables us to state a number of criteria which we shall use to evaluate the continuing relevance of the realist conception of security. From a broadly accepted epistemology we can initially identify these criteria as follows:

- *Consistency* – two aspects of consistency are important: internal and external logics. That is, internally, to what extent does the paradigm provide explanations that are consistent in their internal logic? (This can be approached initially through the formal rules of logic.) Externally, does the paradigm account for the facts of the case being explained?

- *Coherence* – the extent to which any interpretation or account of a social or political phenomenon provides a clearly argued and reasoned narrative.
- *Comprehensiveness* – the extent to which a paradigm accounts for the available facts and how many facts remain to be explained.
- *Scope* – to what extent can a paradigm explain new or changing situations and phenomena which were not included in its original assumptions?[15]

It is in the realm of comprehensiveness and scope that much of the recent critique of the realist conception of security in world politics has taken place. The major theme emanating out of the corpus of recent literature on the subject is a total rejection of the realist concentration on the state at the expense of humanity. A number of recent crises have demonstrated in a dramatic and tragic way the catastrophic insecurity of ordinary people in circumstances where states – and the international system of states – are either unable to provide protection or are themselves the principal sources of violence. Human rights abuses in Burma or Turkey, genocide in Rwanda or Indonesia, and a whole range of outrages against civilians on all sides in the wars of Liberia, Algeria or parts of the former Soviet Union are all cases in point. The conflicts over the remains of Sierra Leone highlight the plight of a population without protection from any state falling prey to the remnants of the very state that was once supposed to be their protector. Equally, the disintegration of the state in Yugoslavia has demonstrated in the most dramatic way the exposure of vast numbers of people not only to the dangers of violence from contending bands of warriors and bandits, in a manner reminiscent of medieval Europe, but also from hunger and disease on a cataclysmic scale. For many people in these societies their chief security threat is the very government under whose sovereignty they live, either through its power and oppressive policies, or as a result of its incapacity to sustain the infrastructure of life for the vast majority.

The recent history of global politics is littered with many instances of how one country or group's national security can be another country or group's insecurity. The apartheid system, which dominated

South African politics for nearly fifty years, provides an illuminating example in this regard. Here we find that, in formal legal terms, the state was constructed as the state of 'the people', of a 'nation' of people. But of course that nationhood was racially qualified: it was a white 'nation', a nation which took racial similarities and hence European origins as the criteria for membership. The state legally validated the white inhabitants of South Africa as sovereign right-bearing subjects who experienced their liberty through their membership of a 'nation' (a nation underpinned by twin ethics of community and brotherhood) and the protection of their rights by the public agency of the state. By so doing the state formally suggested itself to its white subjects as the architectonic political expression of a rational-liberal ethic and security.

The security of the white nations, however, came at the price of insecurity for the native South Africans who were reconstructed as non-nationals. As such, they stood outside the civilized society of the white nation and could not therefore find comfort in the public legal paternalism of the modern liberal state. Many of the apartheid laws sought to reinforce, institutionally as well as ideologically, this reconstructive attitude towards the African majority. Above all, the laws passed by Vorster's government in the 1970s, which set out to make legally viable the reconstitution of the Homelands as a separate 'independent' sovereign state, should be read as an attempt to deny the African majority citizenship of the white nation and hence of security. As Connie Mulder, whom Botha narrowly beat in the 1978 leadership election, put it:

> If our [National Party] policy is taken to its logical conclusion as far as the black people are concerned, there will not be one black [meaning African] man with South African citizenship. Every black man in South Africa will eventually be accommodated in some independent new state in this honourable way and there will no longer be a moral obligation on this parliament to accommodate those people politically.[16]

In other words, the state tried to argue that, in terms of its rational-ethical relations to the white constituency, it represented the ideal security regime. It was on this kind of argument that the state sought to base its claim to the monopoly both of the means of physical violence, and the means of generating an all-encompassing legal-normative order within the borders of the territory of the South African state. Hence, the state presented itself to the white constituents as a state which was just and deserving of obedience because it was a state which, at root, embraced the modern democratic principle of political organization (parliamentary practice, electoral politics, party and caucus dynamics), modern bureaucratic principles of civil administration and modern methods of judicial arbitration. Moreover, the state justified its continued dominance by presenting itself as a form of political order which, in the international realm, would always act reasonably in the interests of the sovereign people in the spheres of economic and military engagement.[17] These were the modern legitimations which the state offered up to the people as arguments which justified its continued dominance. These were also the very arguments which underlined the insecurities of the rest of the black majority.

The new thinking on the concept of security places common humanity rather than *raison d'état* at the core of the normative concerns, implying that security of the state is not necessarily synonymous with the security of everybody living within that state. At the core of the new research agenda for security is the problem of community in world affairs and the nature, development and changeability of principles of moral inclusion and exclusion. This agenda has at least three aspects: the philosophical-normative; the sociological; the practical.[18] The philosophical aspects of inquiry focus on the rationale for the dominant principles of moral exclusion and inclusion in social life, not least the principle of sovereignty providing for the inclusion of citizens and the exclusion of non-citizens. It tends to be chiefly concerned with the reasons for preferring the state, as opposed to the society of states, or the community of humankind as the appropriate vision of community. The emerging literature seeks to broaden the terms of debate further by focusing on other principles of inclusion and exclusion in world affairs associated with class, race, gender, sexual preference and generational difference.

Amidst this growing recognition of diversity and particularism in social life, however, at least some theorists have sought to defend an idea of ethical universalism focused on humanity as a whole. The central issue for this kind of universalism is to find the right balance between the universal and the particular. The sociological aspects of critical international theory are concerned with the historical changeability of principles of moral inclusion and exclusion. They work from the philosophical premise that human moral capacities are not to be presupposed or viewed as given (as, for instance, in the Rawlsian-inspired liberal cosmopolitanism of Charles Beitz, 1979) but must be accounted for within a theory of history. The critical theorist, Andrew Linklater, has identified at least three forms of social learning: learning how to cope with conditions of conflict or strategic rivalry; learning how to manage technological and economic change or technical-instrumental rationalization; learning how to construct forms of order commanding widespread consent (i.e. forms of moral-practical learning). All three forms are both distinct and inter-dependent.[19]

Linklater's work also carries the implication that the history of humanity suggests a contingent capacity to transcend particularistic limitations on freedom and, potentially, the whole spectrum of forms of exclusion. Such a view is complemented by Michael Mann's contention that the various forms of social organizational power have grown, albeit unsteadily, over the course of human history.[20] This insight raises questions as to how developments in social organizational power might be associated with different configurations of social interests and, in turn, changing concepts of community. The practical dimensions of critical international theory focus on the possible aims and strategies of security policies. Such an inquiry examines several key issues: how states might reconcile unilateralist notions of the 'national interest' with the need to maintain international order; how various forms of social learning might condition or require new forms of political collaboration within and across states and, with these, new and more cosmopolitan norms; whether states should promote certain forms of social learning over others; what values and conceptions of world order ought to shape reformist 'national interest'.

This broader and more relative view of security emphasizes the preservation of acquired values rather than the existence or absence of threats, acknowledging that no actor can ever be wholly secure. From this basis, the definition of security may be established through the specification of two factors. The first factor to be specified is a *referent object* – the actor(s) whose security is under discussion. As we have noted, this has traditionally been the nation-state, even though there is nothing inevitable or permanent about defining security in state-centred terms.[21] However, Linklater's framework is equally applicable to the security of other levels of analysis whether the individual, ethnic or religious group, society, state or international system.

Secondly, it is necessary to specify the *values to be protected*, such as political autonomy, territorial integrity or continuity of state identity.[22] Although 'state security' continues to be relevant and states still face challenges to their values of sovereignty and territorial integrity, the changing global landscape has allowed new agendas to emerge and given a greater prominence to other values which relate to other sectors, such as migration, AIDS, environmental and social security. One can distinguish between state security (military, political, economic, environmental) and its concern with threats to its sovereignty, and societal security which relates to existential threats to a cultural identity, particularly in the areas of language, ethnicity and religion. Beyond this, the formulation of a security policy necessitates the specification of further variables, namely: the source of specific threats; the degree of security given to competing objectives; the means and policies for the pursuit of security; the opportunity cost of security for specific values; the time period for a given security policy. It is also important to distinguish between the objective and subjective dimensions of security. While there are often clear differences between what can objectively be assessed as a 'real' threat and what is 'perceived' as such, states and societies may feel insecure without the threat of armed attack – and the perception of threat may be regarded as being as significant as the threat itself. As Waever suggested, there are a number of ways in which groups may perceive their identities as threatened: through the suppression of their expressions (i.e. language, names or dress); through the impeding of their ability to reproduce through the closure of key cultural institutions or exile of members; through competition with other incompatible identities; or through the immigration of 'others'.

This redefinition of the content and purpose of security studies does not entail any attempt to deny or ignore the continuing importance of military security – this would be foolish, particularly in view of recent events in global politics. It does mean, however, that proponents of Critical Security Studies, by placing the poor, the disadvantaged, the voiceless, the under-represented, the powerless at the core of their agenda, recognize that for the majority of the people in the world, apparent 'marginal' or 'esoteric' concerns – such as environmental security, food and economic security – are far more real and immediate threats to their security than interstate wars. This broader conception of security focuses variously, or indeed inter-changeably, on the individual, on society, on civil society, on community, on the continuing integrity of ethnic or cultural groups and on global society. The discourse and practices of security in this context is primarily concerned with the struggle for human emancipation and security.

The 1994 United Nations' Human Development Report gave the new security approach its name and empirical currency. The report referred to the new security agenda collectively as 'Human Security' and assigned its component parts two broad headings: freedom from fear and freedom from want (the key principles underlying the UN Charter itself). Of particular importance, this proposal defined human security as '*people-centred*. It is concerned with how people live and breathe in a society' and argued that 'to address the growing challenge of human security, a new development paradigm is needed that puts people at the centre of development...and respects the natural systems on which all life depends'.[23] Similarly, the 1995 Commission on Global Governance, which emphasizes human security, sets out a list of security objectives that should be of global concern. From its perspective, the principal aims of global security

> should be to prevent conflict and war and to maintain the integrity of the planet's life-support systems by eliminating the economic, social, environmental, political, and military conditions that generate threats to the security of people and the planet, and by anticipating and managing crises before they escalate into armed conflicts.[24]

Poverty and insecurity in southern Africa

In the process of globalization the African continent has quite literally been left behind in terms of the distribution of the spoils of the process. The promised advantages of economic restructuring, as hailed by the IMF, World Bank and individual developed countries, have not been borne out. Foreign investment fails to flow in, debt burdens continue, commodity prices fluctuate, environmental degradation proceeds albeit in a patchy fashion and industrialization fails to occur. Globally, official overseas development aid is falling and foreign direct investment increasing; yet over 66 per cent of the latter went to just eight countries in 1995, none of which were in Africa. Over half of developing countries received little or none.[25] Social and economic polarization are deepening within the continent, urban unemployment has swelled and includes the small middle classes as well as the unskilled workforce; education and health services have been eroded. Literally millions of people are on the move, either internally displaced or as political refugees or economic migrants. The economic and social conditions of the continent exemplify wider global trends of social and economic polarization. Three trends in recent global history seem to be particularly responsible for this;

- Development strategies have concentrated almost exclusively on economic growth, taking no account of the need to ensure the renewal of the environment or the conditions for human survival. The widening economic gap, especially unemployment, is making the structure of society increasingly fragile.
- The end of the cold war and the dismantling of the power blocs has allowed conflicts which were formerly contained in the context of East–West confrontation to erupt openly and with great brutality.
- The end of the East–West division of the world has opened up national economies, allowing for a freer exchange of goods, services and capital. This has stepped up international competition between companies, with constant pressure to increase efficiency by means of labour-saving production technologies and highly developed 'lean management' methods.

If we remove territorial boundaries from our cognitive map, we are left with the picture of people across the African continent attempting to pursue security within the hostile and unpredictable environment of the global capitalist economy. Households are attempting to secure their basic needs in conditions of extreme adversity, as governments and state managers either fail to or are unable to pursue policies which will increase the human security of their citizens. The ability of governments to play a mediatory role between global capitalism and the domestic, intra-state arena is being transformed in an uneven manner, as states exhibit different capacities and different resources as well as different levels of social and political motivation.

The best composite measure of the state of human development is perhaps the UNDP's Human Development Index (HDI), which is widely utilized in its various Human Development Reports. The most striking observation about Africa that emerges out of the HDI ranking is the continent's extremely low level of human development. There are only ten countries in the medium category, including South Africa and Botswana (Algeria, Botswana, Egypt, Gabon, Libya, Mauritius, Morocco, Seychelles, Swaziland and South Africa).[26] Five of them (Mauritius, Seychelles, Botswana, Gabon and Swaziland) have a combined population of 4.6 million. When Libya and Tunisia are added, the figure rises to 17.9 million. All the remaining 41 countries are in the low human development category. This, however, does not tell the entire story. There are 55 countries in this category, which means Africa accounts for 79 per cent of the category. Even more telling is that of the 30 countries with the lowest human development indices, 25 (or 83 per cent) are African.[27] In other words, Africa is the continent with the poorest showing in human development.

Within southern Africa the average life expectancy is 50 years, among the lowest of all regions on the continent. The situation with respect to health, food and nutrition is equally bad. The percentages of the population having access to health services, safe water and sanitation are 59, 45 and 31, respectively, and average calorie supply per capita is only 92 per cent of requirements. In the sphere of education, only 49 per cent of adults can read and write while the enrolment ratio for all levels is 35 per cent, suggesting a very low level of human capital formation. At US$1250, real GDP per capita is among the lowest in the world, and GNP per capita ($540) is extremely low, compared to an average of $880 for all developing countries and $4160 for the world as a whole.[28] Fifty four per cent of the people in the region live in absolute poverty.[29] Critical as the general situation is, it is even worse for children and women. The mortality rates for infants (under 12 months) and children (under five years) are, at 101 and 160 respectively, the highest of all regions. The percentages of children who are underweight, wasted and stunted are 31, 13 and 44 respectively. Trained medical personnel attend only 40 per cent of births and only 49 per cent of one-year-olds are fully immunized.[30]

The situation of southern African women is much worse than that of men. Thus the literacy rate of women is only 60 per cent of that of men and the corresponding figure for mean years of schooling is 40 per cent.[31] Similarly, the gaps in school enrolment are also wide, the figures being 85 per cent, 67 per cent and 35 per cent for primary, secondary and tertiary level education, respectively. While the life expectancy of women is higher than that of men, other indicators of health are biased against women. The maternal mortality rate is 700 per 100 000 live births, and only 64 per cent of women get prenatal care. Women constitute only 33.9 per cent of the labour force. Interestingly, this critical human situation is complicated by obvious imbalances in resource allocation. The share of military expenditure in the GDP, which was 0.7 per cent in 1960, had risen to 3 per cent by 1991. As a percentage of health/education expenditure, military expenditure rose from 27 per cent in 1977 to 43 per cent in 1991. These trends are contrary to what is observed in the developing countries as a group and also in industrial countries. In developing countries military expenditure as a percentage of GDP dropped from 4.2 per cent in 1960 to 3.5 per cent in 1990–91 and as a percentage of combined education and health expenditure from 143 per cent to 600 per cent for the same periods. For the industrial countries, these figures showed a decline from 6.3 per cent to 3.4 per cent and from 97 per cent to 33 per cent respectively.[32]

The overall trends in human development have been positive in some respects. Thus, life expectancy has increased from 40 to 50 years and infant mortality declined from 165 to 101 per 1000 births between 1960 and 1998. Likewise, there has been an increase in adult literacy from 28 to 51 per cent and in primary school enrolment between 1970 and 1990. And there was an increase in the percentage of the population having access to safe water between 1975 and 1998. But these developments have not been of a magnitude great enough to make an appreciable dent in southern Africa's formidable array of social problems. In fact, in certain instances, the situation has grown much worse. For example, in many countries per capita expenditure on health and education has been declining. There have also been reversals in school enrolment ratios and increases in school dropout rates relative to the appreciable gains made in the 1960s and 1970s. Environmental degradation has proceeded unabated and many countries in the region are racked by internal conflicts of one sort or another. The impact of these developments is more adverse on children, women and vulnerable groups. Such trends cry out to be reversed. What is particularly disturbing is that poverty has been increasing at an alarming rate and is projected to increase further. For the wider continent, it is estimated that its share in global poverty is expected to double from 16 per cent in the mid-1980s to 32 per cent.

While it is true that most southern African states are responding to the external pressures of the international financial institutions, their governments still bear responsibility for promoting an approach to development which in its adulation of all things modern sometimes fails to understand and value African socio-economic systems which have evolved over generations. Some such systems have evolved to manage the risks inherent in pursuing self-sufficiency in harsh climatic conditions. The simple but important point is that, just as all things modern are not necessarily helpful in human security terms, all things traditional are not necessarily unhelpful. Attention to specifics is important.

The international financial institutions have been instrumental in promoting the idea that it is common sense or natural that we are reaching the end of history where the free market gains universal acceptance as the legitimate form of economic organization with its attendant social and political relations. Wealth created by the rich will trickle down to the poor. These institutions have also developed an interest in good governance, so we see the pursuit of political liberalization at the same time as economic liberalization.[33] In southern Africa this has created many problems, and it cannot be assumed that economic liberalization is supportive of political liberalization; indeed, the opposite may be true in some cases. The adverse consequences of economic liberalization can undermine the consolidation of democracy. There are plenty of examples of where economic liberalization has contributed directly to anarchy and civil wars, such as in Mozambique, Angola and Lesotho, or simply to political unrest and instability. Riley and Parfitt argue that the deprivations experienced by certain groups who 'have been deprived of their stake in society by some aspect of an austerity programme that has moved them towards or below the poverty line' result in violence.[34] For example, state employees who have been laid off become more critical of the regime and become actively opposed to the economic policies which they see as disadvantaging them. Thus, they argue that the overall result of such economic policies is often 'to destabilise the recipient states as key groups in the populace rebel against the combination of rising prices and declining real wages and public services'.[35]

Structural adjustment policies (SAPs) have done little to foster the social, political and economic conditions that could contribute to the development of stable state–society relations in the region and the creation of a stable social order so vital to the enjoyment of human security. The promotion of exports for debt repayment and the cutting of public expenditure on welfare in a region where 100 million people are undernourished,[36] where there is one doctor for 36 000 people compared with one for 400 people in industrial countries, and where nine out of the 15 million HIV-infected people worldwide reside is a scandal.[37] One author has even referred to SAPs as a form of economic genocide. 'When compared to genocide in various periods of colonial history, its impact is devastating. Structural adjustment programmes directly affect the livelihood of more than four billion people.'[38]

While the voluminous assessments of SAPs fall into two broad camps, those who believe the policies can be reformed and those who think they must be transformed, there is at least broad agreement that SAPs often put the poor at risk. However, the poor are not an undifferentiated group. For example, in some cases there may be greater negative consequences for the urban rather than rural poor. The former rely more on subsidies and government services, employment and so forth, than the latter. Aware of criticism of SAPs, in 1987 the World Bank introduced a 'Social Dimensions of Adjustment' programme.[39] Ghana's SAP was the first in Africa to formally integrate a 'Programme of Actions to Mitigate the Social Costs of Adjustment' or PAMSCAD, on the joint initiative of the government, the World Bank and UNICEF. The jury is still out on the results of this initiative.[40]

HIV/AIDS and southern Africa's future

The HIV virus represents one of the most pressing challenges to human security facing southern African governments at the turn of the new millennium. Globally, the spread of HIV/AIDS has exceeded the worst projections by far. Nearly 34 million people in the world are currently living with the virus and one-third of these are young people between the ages of 10 and 24. The epidemic continues to grow, as 16 000 people worldwide become newly infected each day.[41] Fourteen million adults and children have already lost their lives to this devastating disease, and the death toll rises each year.[42] Despite these alarming figures, AIDS is still an emerging and growing epidemic. The region most affected has been sub-Saharan Africa (SSA). At the end of 1998, 22.5 million people, including 1 million children, were living with HIV/AIDS in SSA, two-thirds of the world-wide total.[43] At least 4 million Africans were newly infected with the virus in 1998.[44]

Decosas and Adrien estimate that deaths due to HIV/AIDS in Africa will soon surpass the 20 million Europeans killed by the plague epidemic of 1347–51.[45] It is estimated that only 10 per cent of the illness and death that this epidemic will bring has been seen. The real impact on people, communities and economies is still to come. Its transmission is often facilitated by subregional trade routes and other migration patterns common throughout the continent. In Botswana, Namibia, Zambia and Zimbabwe, between 20 and 26 per cent of people ages 15 to 49 are infected. In 12 other SSA countries, including Ethiopia, Kenya, Mozambique, South Africa and Tanzania, 9 to 20 per cent of adults are infected.[46] Some countries in West and Central Africa have been less affected and have been able to maintain low and stable HIV infection rates (see Table 5.1). This is due, in part, to an early response to the threat of the epidemic in some countries, and in part because a less virulent HIV strain (HIV-2) predominates in these countries. However, there is no single factor, or clear-cut group of factors, that determines the severity of a country's HIV/AIDS epidemic. There is no affordable cure or vaccine likely to be available in developing countries for a decade or more. The only options are to prevent further spread of the epidemic, minimize its impact and provide a caring and compassionate environment for those infected and affected. This crisis calls for an expanded and

Table 5.1   Adult (15–49) HIV/AIDS prevalence rates, sub-Saharan Africa, 1997

Rank	Country	Adult HIV/ AIDS rate %	Rank	Country	Adult HIV/ AIDS rate %
1	Zimbabwe	25.84	23	Gabon	4.25
2	Botswana	25.10	24	Nigeria	4.12
3	Namibia	19.94	25	Liberia	3.65
4	Zambia	19.07	26	Eritrea	3.17
5	Swaziland	18.50	27	Sierra Leone	3.17
6	Malawi	14.92	28	Chad	2.72
7	Mozambique	14.17	29	Ghana	2.38
8	South Africa	12.91	30	Guinea-Bissau	2.25
9	Rwanda	12.75	31	The Gambia	2.25
10	Kenya	11.64	32	Angola	2.12
11	Central African Republic	10.77	33	Niger	2.09
12	Djibouti	10.30	34	Guinea	2.09
13	Côte d'Ivoire	10.06	35	Benin	2.06
14	Uganda	9.51	36	Senegal	1.77
15	Tanzania	9.42	37	Mali	1.67
16	Ethiopia	9.31	38	Eqt. Guinea	1.21
17	Togo	8.52	39	Mauritania	0.52
18	Lesotho	8.35	40	Somalia	0.25
19	Burundi	8.30	41	Comoros	0.14
20	Congo	7.78	42	Madagascar	0.12
21	Burkina Faso	7.17	43	Mauritius	0.08
22	Cameroon	4.89	44	Seychelles	0.01

Source: UNAIDS (1998a) *Report on the Global HIV/AIDS Epidemic*. Geneva, June.

intensified response to mobilize governments, civil society, the private sector and the international community to take action, increase resources and build capacity to sustain efforts to slow the spread of the epidemic.

The HIV/AIDS epidemic is not only the most important public health problem affecting large parts of SSA, but is an unprecedented threat to the region's development. It is, therefore, a development crisis. The most disturbing long-term feature of the HIV/AIDS epidemic is its impact on life expectancy, making HIV an unprecedented catastrophe in the world's history. Among 18 countries in SSA that experienced a declining or stagnating life expectancy during 1990–98, all but one (Togo) were described as having a generalized HIV/AIDS epidemic, that is an HIV prevalence of more than 5 per cent in the adult population.[47] Conversely, of 29 countries that experienced an improvement in life expectancy, only two, Mozambique and Lesotho, had a generalized epidemic.[48] In nine African countries with adult prevalence of 10 per cent or more, HIV/AIDS will erase 17 years of potential gains in life expectancy, meaning that instead of reaching 64 years, by 2010–15 life expectancy in these countries will *regress* to an average of just 47 years; this represents a reversal of most development gains of the past 30 years – affecting an entire generation.[49]

One unenviable statistical fact is that HIV/AIDS prevalence in southern Africa is the highest of all the regions on the continent. Of the ten most infected African countries eight are located in southern Africa (Table 5.1). Zimbabwe is especially hard hit with up to 50 per cent of pregnant women in some sites infected. In Botswana, Namibia and Zambia, the prevalence rates among pregnant women are between 20 and 40 per cent. South Africa trailed behind many of its neighbours in 1990 but is rapidly catching up (see Chapter 2). The majority of new infections are in young people – those between the ages of 15 and 24 (sometimes younger). Thus in Zambia in one recent study over 12 per cent of the 15–16 year olds seen at an ante-natal clinic were HIV positive. In 1998, South Africa accounted for over half of all new infections in southern Africa and for one in seven new infections in SSA. The percentage of pregnant 15–19 year olds infected with HIV rose from 13 per cent in 1996 to 20 per cent in 1998. In Botswana the HIV rate for the same group stood at 30 per cent in 1998. The infection rates for young women are significantly higher than they are for boys and young men of the same ages – thus in Malawi it is reported that HIV infection rates of young women are five to six times higher than young men in the age range 15–20.

Multiple causation

In explaining the reasons why the virus is more prevalent in southern Africa than elsewhere, one needs to look at a multiplicity of causality. The most persuasive arguments are centred on widespread poverty, the high prevalence of sexually transmitted diseases (STDs), poorly developed health systems, high levels of circulatory migration and rapid urbanization. The arguments around poverty are highly persuasive. Basically, poverty leads to economic strategies which expose the poor to a higher risk of HIV infection. Thus both men and women will seek out livelihoods which offer the possibility of survival, and this will often require migration from villages to towns and cities in search of work. Doing so often leads to a greater relaxation of traditional sexual norms and, in the case of men particularly, will often lead to sexual activity where they have many partners. Evidence supports the proposition that most married women who are infected with HIV have only a single partner – their husbands. The poor women, especially those who head households, are also often pushed into prostitution to support their families. This exposes such women to risks of infection.

There are many other factors also operating in the case of the poorest. They have generally poor health status which is the outcome of their poverty and their lack of access since childhood to adequate health facilities, basic sanitation and a nutritious diet. In part, this is a matter of access to formal health services but it is much more a matter of environmental conditions (such as poor housing, clean water and poor nutrition). Certainly, the poor health status of both men and women in part explains the more rapid progression from HIV infection to death for those who are infected in Africa compared with rich countries.

The relationship between poverty and infection, while evident, is by no means as conclusive as it might seem. For instance, although the poor account for the highest number of those infected with HIV in southern Africa (as elsewhere in the world) the relationship between poverty and the virus is a very complex one. At the macro level, the relationship is very weak because the vast majority of the global poor remain uninfected with the virus. Furthermore – and this is very important and to some extent reasonably well documented – HIV infection is also high among those who are better educated and highly trained. Hence the relationship between poverty and HIV prevalence is at best a weak one because there are the non-poor who also exhibit risk behaviour which can and does leads to HIV infection.

In the context of the above, quite different factors other than poverty must be operating in the case of the skilled, professional and the well educated to explain their high infection rates. The explanation would seem to lie in the opportunities which are available to those categories of people through their access to income and their position in society which allow them to engage in sexual behaviour which places them and their spouses at risk of HIV infection. A survey conducted for this project among the educated elite of Gaborone (Botswana) supports this point. Of the 200 people who were asked to state a simple 'yes' or 'no' to a question about their sexual behaviour in the previous six months, almost 50 per cent indicated that they had had sex with a partner outside their normal relationship. Another interesting factor which emerged was the relationship between the number of the 'yes' respondents to the above question and mobility. The respondents seemed to be drawn from a pool of employment which included high levels of mobility. It would seem that this was a feature of their lifestyle which provided an additional opportunity for unsafe sex. Certainly for this group, it was not poverty which explained their behaviour but the opposite, nor can their behaviour be attributed to lack of access to education since many have achieved secondary and tertiary level, but would seem to be related to work and leisure patterns, and to high levels of mobility.

Regional impact

While there are some ambiguities about its prevalence in the region, there are no ambiguities at all about its impact on regional societies. The HIV/AIDS epidemic is stretching the capacity of social safety nets to the limit. The numbers of AIDS patients, widows and orphans are growing rapidly. The household impacts begin as soon as a member of the household starts to suffer from HIV-related illness. This results in loss of income of the patient, a substantial increase in household expenditures for medical expenses and other members of the household, usually daughters and wives, missing school or work to care for the sick person. Death results not only in additional expenses for funeral and mourning costs, but in a permanent loss of income from less labour on the farm or from lower remittances. Poor households are more vulnerable to the impact of an AIDS death, which significantly affects food expenditure and consumption and ultimately impacts on childhood nutrition.[50] Death of a parent often results in removal of children from school to save educational expenses and increase household labour, resulting in a severe loss of future earning potential. Widows in particular may have no means to support themselves after their husbands die, often forcing them into commercial sex work and increasing their risk of infection. The large number of orphans in southern Africa is not only a major development problem; the increasing number of child-headed house-holds is creating a new social system with inherent problems that societies have yet to address. This growing crisis is putting pressure on regional governments to increasingly support safety nets where they exist or create effective social safety nets where they do not.

With the exception of South Africa (and to a lesser extent Zimbabwe) agriculture is the largest sector in the regional economies, accounting for a large portion of production and employing the majority of workers. The impact of the virus on southern Africa's agricultural industry is already enormous. A study conducted with the Zimbabwe Farmers' Union showed that the death of a bread-winner due to AIDS will cut the production of maize in small-scale farming and communal areas by 61 per cent.[51] In Malawi, where 10 per cent of gross domestic product comes from estate agriculture, the strongest effect of HIV/AIDS will be the negative impact on the supply of skilled labour. The loss of adults to AIDS often leads to a shift in cropping patterns. In many cases, this means switching from subsistence farming to cash crops. It can also reduce investments in soil enhancement, irrigation and other capital improvements, which have long-term impacts on output. AIDS forces families to make irreversible decisions to sell livestock, equipment and land to cover AIDS-related expenses, leaving surviving family members in poverty from which it is hard to escape.[52]

The overall level of impact of the virus on the region is not yet clear. What is certain is that inaction will cost the region dearly. Although prevention strategies were known early in the course of the epidemic and many interventions have been implemented on a limited scale, none of the regional states have taken sufficient action to curtail the spread of HIV/AIDS. Inaction to date has resulted in millions of new infections and unnecessary deaths, leading to the current crisis situation. More than 2 million people in the region were infected in 1998, and the numbers are certainly on the increase. The resulting social decay and community breakdown will threaten not only the socio-economic development of regional states, but also their political stability. Regional health systems are stretched beyond their limits as they not only deal with a growing number of AIDS patients and the loss of health personnel due to death and illness, but also cope with rising cases of tuberculosis, the most common opportunistic infection associated with AIDS. In Zambia and Zimbabwe,

HIV-infected patients occupy 50 to 80 per cent of all beds in urban hospitals. The services provided meet only a fraction of the needs. Yet spending on AIDS care is crowding out spending on other life-saving, cost-effective programmes. On average, treating an AIDS patient for one year is about as expensive as educating ten primary school students for one year.[53] There is little hope that any development goals for health (e.g. reduced infant, child and maternal mortality; reduced mortality from malaria) can be achieved in the face of AIDS. The motivation and incentive system for health workers needs to be reviewed from the perspectives of both service delivery and overall sectoral objectives. AIDS also poses significant challenges for health sector reform and is dramatically changing the disease burden profile in many countries.[54]

Notes

Introduction

1. See L. Nathan (1994) *The Changing of the Guard: Armed Forces and Defence Policy in a Democratic South Africa* (Pretoria: HSRC/RGN Publishers).

2. Larry Swatuk and David Black (eds) (1997) *Bridging the Rift: The New South Africa in Africa* (Boulder, Colo.: Westview Press).

3. Cited from an interview with Professor Davis in Cape Town on 19 March 1996.

4. André du Pisani (1993) 'Post-settlement South Africa and the future of Southern Africa', *Journal of Opinions*, vol. 21, p. 60.

5. SADCC (1992) *SADCC: Towards Economic Integration*, Theme Document for the January 1992 Annual Consultative Conference (Maputo: 29–31 January 1992), p. 10. Also see J. Blumenfeld (1991) *Economic Interdependence in Southern Africa: from conflict to Co-operation* (New York: St. Martin's Press); F. Cheru (1992) 'The not so brave New World: problems and prospects of regional integration in post-apartheid Southern Africa', SAIIA, p. 2; Gavin Maasdorp and Alan Whiteside (eds) (1992) *Towards a Post-Apartheid Future: Political and Economic Relations in Southern Africa*.

6. Cited from an interview with Professor Davies in Cape Town on 19 March 1996.

7. Ibid.

8. Ibid.

9. R. Gilpin (1987) *The Political Economy of International Relations* (Princeton, NJ: Princeton University Press); also see P. Gourevitch (1986) *The Politics of Hard Times: Comparative Responses to International Economic Crises* (Ithaca, NY: Cornell University Press).

10. B. M. Russett, 'The mysterious case of vanishing hegemony: or is Mark Twain really dead?' *International Organization*, vol. 39, 1985, p. 218.

11. A. Lipietz (1987) *Mirages and Miracles* (London: Verso Press) p. 5.

12. S. Hanlon (1986) *Beggar Your Neighbour: Apartheid Power in Southern Africa* (London: Catholic Institute for Industrial Relations/James Currey) This book provides one of the most illuminating examples in this line of thinking.

13. S. Haggard (1990) *Pathway from the Periphery* (Ithaca, NY: Cornell University Press) p. 21.

14. Lipietz, op. cit., p. 3.

15. R. Keohane (ed.) (1986) *Neo-realism and its Critics* (New York: Columbia University Press).

16. It follows that to insist on the primacy of any one 'factor' or 'dimension' in historical interpretation is to unleash a 'ritual without hope or an end' in which scholars fruitlessly seek to advance one view over another. See Mann, *The Sources of Social Power: the History of Power from the Beginning to 1760 AD*, vol. 1 (Cambridge University Press), p. 19.
17. N. Poku (1998) 'Constructivism and Third World Research', *International Relations*, vol. XIV, no. 2, pp. 35–47.
18. N. Onuf (1989) *World of Our Making: Rules and Rule in Social Theory and International Relations* (Columbia: University of South Carolina Press) p. 39.
19. Ibid., p. 43.
20. Ibid., pp. 42–3.
21. Bernstein defines objectivism as some permanent, ahistorical framework to which we can ultimately appeal in determining the nature of rationality, knowledge, truth, reality, goodness and rightness. Relativism, by contrast, he defines as the claim that there can be no higher appeal than to a given conceptual scheme, language game, set of social practices or historical epoch. (See R. Bernstein, *Beyond Relativism and Objectivism: Science, Hermeneutics and Praxis* (Oxford: Basil Blackwell, 1983) pp. 8–11).
22. This discussion of structurationism is focused principally on the work of its prime exponent Anthony Giddens, general commentary thereupon and recent discussion of theory in International Relations.
23. A. Giddens (1984) *The Constitution of Society: Outline of a Theory of Structuration* (Oxford: Polity Press) p. 374.
24. In the light of the claim to reflexivity advanced above, one key question which a discussion of structurationism prompts is how it has gained such prominence in current social theory. One answer is that it engages difficult and recurring questions in social ontology in novel ways. Central to this is the way structurationism reflects the influence of the current 'post' or 'late' modern mentality which accepts that there is no fixed reality, touchstone of truth, secure foundations or Archimedean point on which to ground an objective reason. Such a view embodies a new appreciation of the centrality of contingency in social life. Agnes Heller has expressed the sensibility thus: 'Contingency is not a philosophical construct which could be replaced by any other constructs but the life experience of the modern individual, a vexing, threatening but also promising experience (termed by Kierkegaard the experience of possibility and anxiety)', in A. Heller (1988) 'The moral situation in modernity', *Social Research*, vol. 55, pp. 531–50. This notion of contingency implies not only the endogeneity of all social institutions but also the contingent way the human subject's knowledge and identity are co-constituted with social reality. Such a conception of the reflexive agent's relationship with social institutions is central to structurationism which, in turn, can be understood as an ontology of contingency. An appreciation of this suggests, as Giddens himself has argued, a radical new phase of modernity in which all institutions come to be viewed as potentially revisable on a global scale.

25. Onuf has insightfully elaborated the point thus: 'Human agents author rules and deploy resources in accordance with those rules so as to secure and ensconce advantages over other agents. Their differential success produces asymmetries in the ability of agents to control the actions of other agents in time and space as well as the possibility that disadvantaged but competent agents can subvert or reverse such asymmetries' (Onuf, op. cit., p. 60).

26. See M. Mann (1986) *The Sources of Social Power: the History of Power from the Beginning to 1760 AD*, vol. 1 (Cambridge: CUP).

27. Giddens does not make this connection directly because he has, as Bernstein points out, failed to deal adequately with the relationship between structurationism and critical theory. In part, this reflects his suspicion about any attempt to 'ground' critique. But as Bernstein also points out we do not have to endorse some unqualified universalist, ahistorical, hegemonic or 'bad' foundationalism to find common as well as divergent bases for a contingent, historically situated critical wisdom or gesture among the different forms of social science and social understanding. As Heller has noted: '[i]t is ill conceived to establish a direct relation between the increasing relativism of worldviews (philosophies) and the relativism of morals. Perhaps the opposite is the case: [t]hrough absolutizing their own philosophies and worldviews, philosophers contribute more to the relativisation of morals, even boosting nihilism, than by acceptance of the mutual relativisation of their philosophical enterprises, by finding only a single and restricted common ground: a few moral norms and values which might be regarded as valid and binding for all of us. The diversity of worldviews ... does not bar the emergence of a common ethos, unless one of the competing worldviews determines the commandments and the interdictions completely, and does so not only for its own adherents but also with a universalising aspiration' (Heller, op. cit., pp. 538–9).

28. Rob Walker has expressed the rationale for such a claim well: 'To engage with the literature on the emergence and development of the states-system is to be impressed by the transformative quality of both the state and the character of relations between states. States can then appear to us as historically constituted and always subject to change.' See R. B. J. Walker (1989) 'History and method in international relations', *Millennium*, vol. 18, pp. 163–83.

29. See, for example, Escobar's work: A. Escobar (1995) *Encountering Development* (Princeton, NJ: Princeton University Press). Also, see D. Apter (1996) *Rethinking Development: Modernisation, Dependency, and Postmodern Politics* (London: Sage Press).

30. For example, P. Katzenstein (1985) *Small States in World Markets* (Ithaca, NY: Cornell University Press) pp. 136–7; Hall, op. cit., pp. 259–60; and S. Strange (1988) *States and Markets: An Introduction to International Political Economy* (London: Pinter).

31. For example, R. Cox (1987) *Power, Production and World Order* (New York: Colombia University Press) and Walker op. cit.

Chapter 1   Southern Africa: Colonialism and Its Legacies

1. The British High Commissioner in South Africa, Sir Alfred Milner, on the question of African enfranchisement in 1905, quoted in *Frontiers*, 1962, vol. 2, p. 1273.
2. Nana Poku and Lloyd Pettiford (eds) (1998) *Redefining Security* (London: Macmillan) p. 199.
3. B. Davidson (1992) *The Black Man's Burden: Africa and the curse of the Nation-State* (London: James Currey) p. 121.
4. Diaries of Lieutenant Patrick Forbes, cited in Davidson, ibid., p. 22.
5. P. Gifford and W. R. Louis (1971) *France and Britain in Africa: Imperial Rivalry and Colonial Rule* (New Haven, CT: Yale University Press).
6. See A. G. Hopkins (1973) *An Economic History of West Africa* (Harlow: Longman).
7. With serious implications witnessed up to the present day. Unfortunately, word space does not allow for any serious analysis of this particular group within the context of this chapter. A useful introduction to the subject is provided by Gerhard Mare (1992) *Ethnicity and Politics in South Africa* (London: Zed Books).
8. C. W. de Kiewet, 'A history of South Africa: social and economic', quoted in F. Vorheis, (1990) 'From colonial mercantilism to nationalism and socialism in Africa', *South African Journal of Economic History*, vol. 5, no. 2, p. 117.
9. Germanic influence is evident in parts of present-day areas of Namibia and Tanzania. Portugal played a role in the subcontinent in Angola and Mozambique. Britain, the most influential ex-colonial power, controlled at its peak the modern-day areas of Botswana, Lesotho, Malawi, South Africa, Swaziland, Zambia and Zimbabwe.
10. T. R. H. Davenport (1988) *South Africa: A Modern History* (Johannesburg: Southern). This treaty (1891) also guaranteed rail access to the Mozambican port of Beira for British settlers in the interior and aided creeping British colonialization of the interior. The British government, therefore, gained better sea access to a greater area, treating the region as a whole instead of as individual territories. See R. Reinhardt (1984) 'Historical setting', in H. Nelson (ed.), *Mozambique: A Country Study* (Washington, DC: American University).
11. E. Axelson (1967) *Portugal and the Scramble for Africa* (Johannesburg: Wits University Press) p. 18.
12. Ibid., p. 16.
13. Reinhardt, op. cit., pp. 37–8.
14. The Anglo-German Treaty of 1890 and the Anglo-Portuguese Treaty of 1891 were the result of conflicting colonial aspirations. For the colonial powers to have entered into conflict over tracts of remote territory would have been extremely costly so these matters were resolved diplomatically.

15. Quoted by G. S. Labuschagne (1969) *Suid-Afrika en Afrika: Die staatkundige verhouding in die tydperk 1945–1966* (Cape Town: Sentrum vir Internasionle Polititie), p. 16.
16. Quoted by J. C. Smuts Jr (1952) *Jan Smuts* (London: Cassell) p. 447.
17. See S. C. Nolutshungu, (1975) *South Africa in Africa: A Study in Ideology and Foreign Policy* (Manchester: Manchester University Press).
18. During Malan's tenure as Prime Minister (1948–54) the foundations of apartheid were laid with the enactment of the Prohibition of Mixed Marriages Act 1949, the Immorality Act 1950 and the Group Areas Act 1950.
19. South Africa, Debate of the House of Assembly (Hansard), 1/9/1948, cols. 1325 and 1326;1949. cols. 5661 and 5662.
20. House of Assembly Debates, vol. 52, col. 3956, in Nolutshungu, op. cit., p. 46.
21. D. J. Geldenhuys (1977) 'The Effects of South Africa's Racial Policy on Anglo-South African Relations 1945–1961'. Unpublished PhD dissertation, p. 242.
22. Ibid., p. 241.
23. Labuschagne, op. cit., p. 26.
24. Geldenhuys, op. cit., p. 269.
25. Quoted by J. Barber (1973) *South Africa's Foreign Policy 1945–1970* (Oxford: Oxford University Press) p. 106.
26. Hansard Debate, 27/l/1959, cols. 62 and 63; 20/51959, col. 6227.
27. Hansard Debate, 4/5/1959, cols. 5254 and 5255, and South African Department of Information, Dr H. F. Verwoerd, *Crisis in World Conscience II. The Road to Freedom for Basutoland, Bechuanaland, Swaziland,* Fact Paper 106, undated, pp. 14–15.
28. Quoted by T. D. Venter (1976) '"Confederation Association of States or Federation?" A future political dispensation for South and southern Africa: theoretical perspectives for South African party politics', *South African Journal of African Affairs*, nos. 1 and 2, p. 137.
29. Quoted ibid.
30. R. Hyam (1972) *The Failure of South Africa's Expansion, 1908–1948* (London: Macmillan) pp. 47–71.
31. Quoted by G. M. Cockram (1970) *Vorster's Foreign Policy* (Pretoria: Academia) p. 186.
32. Ibid., p. 131.
33. Ibid., pp. 163–6.
34. Ibid., pp. 164–5.
35. Ibid.
36. Ibid., p. 126.
37. Barber, op. cit., p. 231.
38. See C. J. Barratt (1971) *A Dialogue in Africa* (Johannesburg: SAIIA) p. 23.
39. Hansard Debate, 4/2/1974, cols. 59 and 60.
40. South Africa, Senate Debate, 23/10/1974, cols. 3340–6.
41. On détente, see C. Legum (1976) *Vorster's Gamble for Africa: How the Search for Peace Failed* (London: Rex Collings) pp. 11–31.
42. Ibid., p. 12.

43. D. J. Geldenhuys (1979) *The Neutral Option and Sub-continental Solidarity: A Consideration of Foreign Minister Pik Botha's Zurich Statement of 7 March 1979*, Occasional Paper (Johannesburg: SAIIA) pp. 4–5.
44. Hansard Debate, 3/4/1979, col. 3919.
45. See Address by the Hon. R. F. Botha, South African Minister for Foreign Affairs, to Ministers and Guests of the Swiss–South African Association in Zurich on 7 March 1979, Press Section, S. A. Embassy, Berne, pp. 17 and 25.
46. Address by the Honourable P. W. Botha, Prime Minister.
47. Hansard Debate, 5/6/1979, col. 7801.
48. Hansard Debate, 6/6/1979, col. 7940.
49. Address by the Honourable P. W. Botha, Carlton Centre, Johannesburg, 22 November 1979, issued by the South African Department of Foreign Affairs.
50. J. A. Lombard (1978) *Freedom, Welfare and Order* (Pretoria: Benbo) p. 191.
51. Carlton speech, op. cit., pp. 7–14.
52. Tony Rand, *Daily Mail*, 23 November 1979.
53. Republic of South Africa, Department of Defence, White Paper on Defence and Armament Supply 1979, p. iii (prefaced by P. W. Botha).
54. Hansard Debate, 6/6/1979, col. 7940.
55. D. J. Geldenhuys (1984) *The Diplomacy of Isolation: South Africa's Foreign Policy Making* (London: Macmillan) p. 145.
56. D. O'Meara (1986) 'Destabilisation in southern Africa: total strategy in total disarray', *Monthly Review*, vol. 7, no. 1, p. 54.
57. UN ECA (1989) *South African Destabilization: The Economic Costs of Frontline Resistance to Apartheid* (New York: UN Economic Commission for Africa).

Chapter 2   South Africa: from Apartheid to Democracy

1. See D. O'Meara (1983) *Volkapitalism: Class, Capital and Ideology in the Development of Afrikaner Nationalism, 1934–1948* (Cambridge: Cambridge University Press).
2. S. Greenburg (1980) *Race and State in Capitalist Development: Comparative Perspectives* (New Haven, CT and London: Greenwood Press).
3. See H. Wolpe (1972) 'Capitalism and cheap labour power in South Africa: from segregation to apartheid', *Economy and Society*, vol. 1, no. 4, pp. 52–71.
4. R. H. Davies (1979) *Capital, State and White Labour in South Africa, 1900–1960: An Historical Materialist Analysis of Class Formation and Class Relations* (Atlantic Highlands, NJ: Humanities Press).
5. Cf. ibid., Appendix A, pp. 273–7. There were of course certain communist overtones to this charter, including the idea that 'the land shall be shared among those who work it', overtones which again qualify the kind of modernity the ANC was trying to pursue. Mandela's government tried to distance itself from such communist qualifiers, largely because it did not want to alienate potential foreign investors.

6. Ibid., p. 14.
7. In April 1960 the UN Security Council passed Resolution 4300 (with Britain and France abstaining), which called for an end to apartheid. In November 1962 the UN General Assembly passed resolution 1761 calling upon members separately or collectively in conformity with the Charter, among other articles of international law, to break diplomatic relations with South Africa and to boycott South African trade.
8. The UN resolved to institute a trade boycott in 1962, i.e. in the immediate aftermath of the Sharpeville massacre. Indeed sanctions were in many ways a direct response to the internal anti-apartheid movement's cry for international support for their project. Thus even in 1990, on a visit to America, Nelson Mandela maintained the long-running ANC tradition to secure the continuation of sanctions against South Africa – see Guy Arnold (1992) *South Africa – Crossing the Rubicon* (New York: St. Martin's Press), p. 136. According to T. R. H. Davenport, 'if a single event can be said to have committed the international community to a general sanctions policy it was Botha's "Rubicon" speech of August 1985, for the false expectations it aroused after the outbreak of the disturbances of that year, seen against the continuing deadlock in South West Africa and the unstable relation between South Africa and the Frontline states' (*South Africa: a Modern History*. London: Macmillan, 1991, p. 463).
9. J. Suckling and W. Landeg (eds) (1988) *After Apartheid: Renewal of the South African Economy*. (London: Centre for Southern African Studies; University of York in association with James Currey), p. 1.
10. SADCC Annual Report, 1987, p. 9.
11. SADCC Annual Report, 1996, p. 13.
12. Earl A. McFarland Jr (1983) 'The benefits to the RSA of her exports to the BLS countries', in M. A. Oommen et al. (eds), *Botswana's Economy since Independence* (New Delhi: Tata McGraw-Hill).
13. The first customs union in what is present-day South Africa was established in 1989, and by 1995 it had grown to cover the entire area of what are today South Africa, Botswana, Lesotho and Swaziland and the newly independent Namibia (BLSN). The organization provides for the duty-free movement of goods and services between member states and also for a common external tariff against the rest of the world, but also goes beyond a purely customs union in that it includes excise duties as well. The revenue-sharing formula contains a compensation factor of 42 per cent for BLSN. The amounts so calculated are then amended by a stabilization factor aimed at guaranteeing to each BLSN country a rate of revenue of between 17 and 23 per cent. The Customs Union Commission meets annually, but SACU has no office or staff: it is handled by government departments in each member state while the common revenue pool is managed by the South African Reserve Bank. Until 1976 – when Botswana withdrew – all five were also members of the Common (or Rand) Monetary Area (CMA). For historical reasons, an important feature of SACU is that no member state may enter into

a concessionary trade agreement with an outside country unless its partners agree.

14. As reported by Ted Adland, Chairman of the Federated Chamber of Industries Technology Development Committee (*Cape Times*, 15 November 1989). No official figures are available for the latter part of the 1980s.

15. *The Star* (International Airmail Edition), 8 February 1990, quoting then Trade Minister, Kent Durr.

16. *The Star*, 28 January, 1992.

17. See SADCC Annual Report, 1986.

18. Commonwealth Committee of Foreign Ministers on South Africa (1989) *South Africa: The Sanctions Report* (London: Penguin) chapter 3.

19. For a discussion of the use of alternative mechanisms for the transfer of technology to South Africa – and for case studies of the automobile and telecommunications sectors – see R. Kaplinsky (1989) *Sanctions Against South Africa*, Report Prepared for the United Nations Center on Transnational Corporations (New York: UNCTC).

20. It is of interest that these countries also reduced their exports to South Africa by $0.88 billion in the same period. See Commonwealth Committee, op. cit., p. 39.

21. Keith Ovenden and Tony Cole (1989) *Apartheid and International Finance: A Programme for Change* (Victoria, Australia; Harmondsworth: Penguin Books).

22. A. Brink (1996) *Reinventing a Continent* (London: Secker & Warburg) p. 4.

23. Ibid., p. 4.

24. F. Cheru (1997) 'Civil society and political economy in South and Southern Africa', in Stephen Gill (ed.), *Globalization, Democratization and Multilateralism* (London: Macmillan) p. 226.

25. P. J. McGowan (1996) 'The "New" South Africa: ascent or descent in the world system?', in C. Roe Goddard et al. (eds), *International Political Economy: State-Market Relations in the Changing Global Order* (London: Lynne Rienner).

26. Cited in Suckling and Landeg, op. cit., p. 1.

27. SADCC Annual Report, 1987, p. 9.

28. SADC Annual Report, 1996, p. 13.

29. African Development Bank (1997) *Economic Integration in Southern Africa* (Abidjan: ADB) p. 249.

30. See Pieter Esterhuysen (1995) *Africa at a Glance 1995/96: Facts and Figures* (Pretoria: African Institute of South Africa) pp. 42–3.

31. South African Reserve Bank (1995a) *Quarterly Bulletin*, no. 195, March, p. 21.

32. South African Reserve Bank (1995b) *Quarterly Bulletin*, no. 197, September.

33. See S. Gelb (ed.) (1991) *South Africa's Economic Crisis* (London: Zed Books). See also Greg Mills, Alan Begg and Anthoni van Nieuwkerk (eds) (1995) *South Africa in the Global Economy* (Johannesburg: SAIIA).

34. Mills et al., op. cit. p. 7.

35. Ibid., p. 5.

36. South African Reserve Bank (1997a) *Annual Economic Report 1997*, Pretoria.

37. South African Reserve Bank (1997a) *Annual Economic Report 1997*, Pretoria.

38. M. McGrath and A. Whiteford (1994) *Inequality in the size of Distribution in South Africa*, Stellenbosch Economic Project, Occasional Paper, No. 10.

39. According to data from the Central Statistics Service (CSS), the ratio of black to white wages rose from 0.32 in 1989 to 0.37 in 1993.

40. S. Archer, N. Bromberger, N. Nattrass and G. Oldham (1990) 'Unemployment and labour market issues – a beginners guide', in N. Nattrass and E. Ardington (eds), *The Political Economy of South Africa* (Cape Town: Oxford University Press).

41. G. Standing, J. Sender and J. Weeks (1996) *The South African Challenge: Restructuring the Labour Market*, ILO Country Review, Draft Report (Geneva: ILO) p. 99.

42. For a more detailed overview of the industry, see M. Shaw (1995) 'Privatising crime control? South Africa's private security industry', in *Partners in Crime? Crime, Political Transition and Changing Forms of Policing Control* (Johannesburg: Centre for Policy Studies).

43. See M. Shaw (1996) 'The growing threat of Nigerian organised crime in South Africa', *SA Exclusive*, November.

44. M. Shaw (1997) 'Organised Crime in South Africa', unpublished briefing paper, Institute for Security Studies, Halfway House, July.

45. M. Shaw (1997) *South Africa: Crime In Transition*, Institute for Security Studies Occasional Paper No. 17, March.

46. D. Ehlers, I. Hirshfeld and C. Schutte (1996) *Perceptions of Current Sociopolitical Issues in South Africa*, Centre for Sociopolitical Analysis, Human Sciences Research Council, Pretoria, June; this confirms previous survey data. A confidential government poll also drew similar conclusions.

47. Ibid.

48. WHO Address to Marrakesh Conference, 1994. Zimbabwe, *AIDS Information Network News Bulletin*, no. 2, March, pp. 11–12.

49. D. J. Martin, B. D. Schoub, G. N. Padayachee et al. (1990) 'One year surveillance of HIV 1 infection in Johannesburg, South Africa', *Transactions of the Royal Society of Tropical Medicine and Hygiene*, vol. 84, pp. 728–30.

50. N. O'Farrell, I. Windsor and P. Becker (1990) *Risk Factors for HIV 1 Amongst STD Clinic Attenders in Durban, South Africa*. VI International Conference on AIDS, San Francisco, 6/20 24, Poster F. C. 604.

51. RSA Department of National Health and Population Development (1991) *First National HIV Survey of Women Attending Antenatal Clinics, South Africa, October/November 1990, Epidemiological Comments*, vol. 18, no. 2, pp. 35–44. RSA Department of National Health and Population Development (1992), *Second National HIV Survey of Women Attending Antenatal Clinics, South Africa, October/November 1991, Epidemiological Comments*, vol. 19, no. 5, pp. 80–92. RSA Department of National Health and Population Development (1993) *Third National HIV Survey of Women Attending Antenatal Clinics, South Africa, October/November 1992, Epidemiological Comments*, vol. 20, no. 3, pp. 35–50.

52. RSA Department of National Health and Population Development (1994) *Fourth National HIV Survey of Women Attending Antenatal Clinics, South Africa, October/November 1993, Epidemiological Comments*, vol. 21, no. 4, pp. 68–78. RSA Department of National Health and Population Development (1994) *HIV Sentinel Surveillance, Epidemiological Comments*, vol. 21, no. 11, pp. 230–1.

53. RSA Department of National Health and Population Development (1995) *Fifth National HIV Survey in Women Attending Antenatal Clinics of the Public Health Services in South Africa, October/November 1994, Epidemiological Comments*, vol. 22, no. 5, pp. 90–100. RSA Department of National Health and Population Development (1996) *Sixth National HIV Survey of Women Attending Antenatal Clinics of the Public Health Services in the Republic of South Africa, October 1996, Epidemiological Comments*, vol. 23, no. 1, pp. 3–16.

Chapter 3   Regionalization, Integration and Southern Africa

1. The list of nations and regions that are feeling the force of nationalistic pressures is long; an incomplete list includes Canada, the former Yugoslavia, the former Czechoslovakia, the Soviet Union, Great Britain, Germany and almost every country on the African continent.

2. N. Poku and David Graham (eds) (1999) *Population Movements and Human Security* (London: Routledge) chapter 1.

3. An incomplete list includes the formation of the European Free Trade Area (EFTA) in 1960, bilateral arrangements between the United States and Canada under the Auto Pact of 1965 and the 1988 Canada–US Free Trade Agreement, and more recently other initiatives include EU/EFTA negotiations to form the European Economic Area (EEA), Canada–US–Mexico negotiations to form the North American Free Trade Area (NAFTA) and others. A large number of regional integrative arrangements between other countries besides the US and EU have also emerged. They include the Latin American Free Trade Association (LAFTA) of 1960, the Central American Common Market Association (CACM) of 1961, and the East African Common Market (EACM) of the same period. Among the many initiatives to emerge over the past two or so decades on the African continent, the most prominent were the Southern African Development Coordination Conference (SADCC) and the Preferential Trade Area (PTA).

4. A. Etzioni (1965) *Political Unification: A Comparative Study of Leaders and Forces* (New York: Holt, Rinehart & Winston) p. 4.

5. Ibid., p. 8.

6. K. W. Deutsch (1988) *The Analysis of International Integration* (London: Prentice Hall).

7. E. B. Haas (1971) 'The study of regional integration', in L. Lindberg and S. A. Scheingold (eds), *Regional Integration: Theory and Research* (Cambridge, MA: Harvard University Press).

8. B. Hettne (1998) 'Globalization, Regionalism and the New Third World', in Nana Poku and Lloyd Pettiford (eds), *Redefining the Third World* (London: Macmillan).

9. Ibid., p. 73.

10. Bernstein defines objectivism as some permanent, ahistorical framework to which we can ultimately appeal in determining the nature of rationality, knowledge, truth, reality, goodness and rightness. Relativism, by contrast, he defines as the claim that there can be no higher appeal than to a given conceptual scheme, language game, set of social practices, or historical epoch. (See R. Bernstein (1983), *Beyond Relativism and Objectivism: Science, Hermeneutics and Praxis*. Oxford: Basil Blackwell, pp. 8–11.)

11. Ibbo Mandaza, SADCC (1990): 'Problems of regional political and economic cooperation in southern Africa: an overview', cited in A. Nyonyo (ed.), *Regional Integration in Africa. Unfinished Agenda* (Cape Town: David Phillips Press, 1990).

12. See J. Blumenfeld (1991) *Economic Interdependence in Southern Africa: From conflict to Cooperation*, p. 8. (London: Pinter, for Royal Institute of International Affairs).

13. B. Tsie (1996) 'States and markets in the Southern African Development Community (SADC): beyond the neo-liberal paradigm', *Journal of Southern African Studies*, vol. 22, p. 75.

14. Integration in economic literature refers to trade integration among countries. There are four stages of true integration, starting with a free trade area and progressing through a customs union and a common market to an economic union. A free trade area could be preceded by an agreement on preferential tariffs while an economic union could, in theory, develop further into a full political union – see Chapter 2.

15. Cited from an interview with Professor G. Maasdorp, 21 March 1986, Natal, South Africa. Professor Maasdorp was then Head of Political Economy at the University of Natal.

16. Gavin Maasdorp and Alan Whiteside (eds) (1992) *Towards a Post-Apartheid Future: Political and Economic Relations in Southern Africa*. World Bank (1991) *Sub-Saharan Africa: From Crisis to Sustainable Growth*, World Bank Report (Washington, DC: World Bank,) p. 61. N. Mandela, (1993) 'South Africa's future foreign policy', *Foreign Affairs*, vol. 72, November – December, p. 91.

17. World Bank, op. cit., p. 61.

18. Ibid., p. 162.

19. J. Viner, (1950) *The Customs Union Issue* (New York: Carnegie Endowment for International Peace).

20. J. Meade, (1955) *The Theory of Customs Union* (Amsterdam: North Holland).

21. B. Belassa, (1961) *The Theory of Economic Integration* (London: George Allen & Unwin).

22. African Development Bank (1994) *Economic Integration in Southern Africa*, vol. 2, (Oxford: Biddles).

23. P. Robson (1968) *Economic Integration in Africa* (London: George Allen & Unwin) p. 27.

24. Ibid., p. 22.

25. Ibid., p. 27.

26. There is of course the possibility that integration, by allowing the exploitation of comparative advantage, also spurs the emergence of new industries in the least developed regions. Which of these opposite effects of integration on the industrial development of a country will prevail is ultimately an empirical question. The evidence is mixed. On the one hand, experience suggests that countries that have removed trade barriers and integrated with the world at large have also seen the emergence of solid, competitive industries within their national boundaries. The case of South East Asian countries is the most revealing example. On the other hand, the persistence of depressed regions within nations or regional groupings such as the Community suggests that full integration with a geographically limited area may indeed polarize the initial industrial imbalance.

27. L. K. Mytelka (1973) 'The salience of gains in Third-World integrative systems', *World Politics*, vol. 24, pp. 236–50.

28. Ibid., p. 237.

29. Gunnar Myrdal (1957) *Economic Theory and Underdeveloped Regions* (Princeton: Princeton University Press), p. 128.

30. Daniel C. Bach (1983) 'The politics of West African Economic Co-operation: CEAO and ECOWAS', *Journal of Modern African Studies*, vol. 4, pp. 23–36.

31. During 1976 and 1986, for example, it has been calculated that Côte d'Ivoire and Senegal contributed 60.7 and 38.8 per cent respectively to the FCD – ibid., p. 599. It is noteworthy that at least once (1980) during that period, both governments had to call for a postponement of their contributions in the face of serious financial difficulties. – ibid., p. 621.

32. See SADCC Annual Report, 1986.

33. R. Davies (1997), 'South Africa and Southern Africa', paper delivered at a conference on *South and Southern Africa: Lessons from Emerging Markets* (Braamfontein: South African Institute of International Affairs) p. 3.

34. Trade figures and information compiled from the *Monthly Abstract of Trade Statistics*, South African Commissioner for Customs and Excise.

35. Industrial Development Corporation (IDC) (1995) *Impact of Trade Liberalisation on Intra-regional Trade in SADC*, presentation to Workshop on SADC Trade Protocol organized by the Department of Trade and Industry, Pretoria, June.

36. See M. Reitzes (1994) 'Alien issues', *Indicator*, vol. 12, no. 1, and H. Solomon and J. Cilliers (1996) *People, Poverty and Peace: Human Security in Southern Africa*, Halfway House: IDP Monograph Series No. 4, May.

37. Maxi Schoeman and Nana Poku (1999) *Regional Integration in Southern Africa: A Cautionary Note.* Paper delivered at the 39th Convention of the International Studies Association, Washington, DC.

38. E. Adler (1998) 'Condition(s) of peace', *Review of International Studies*, vol. 24 (Special Issue), p. 165.
39. Taylor, op. cit. p. 7.

Chapter 4 Regionalism through institutions: SACU, SADC and COMESA

1. Prior to Namibia's membership, the acronym for Botswana, Lesotho and Swaziland was BLS. Thereafter it became BLSN.
2. These figures are correlated from various UN statistics.
3. As will became apparent later on, in addition to the compensatory formula, this structure will make it impossible for SACU to become the basis for a post-apartheid regional integrative body.
4. *Business Day*, Johannesburg, 2 September 1994, p. 1.
5. Botswana figures have been computed from the Bank of Botswana's Annual Report 1990, pp. 102, 109; Lesotho figures from the Central Bank's Quarterly Review, June 1994, p. 83; Swaziland figures from information provided by the Central Bank of Swaziland.
6. Botswana's economy is heavily oriented towards mining, as reflected in the fact that the percentage of diamonds, copper and nickel of total exports increased from an annual average of 71.2 per cent over the period 1990–95 to 87 per cent over the period 1996-99. (Cited from the Bank of Botswana's Annual Report, 1999, p. 99.)
7. Ibid., p. 80.
8. This information has been taken from the *Swaziland Annual Statistical Bulletin*, 1989, p. 4.
9. Maasdorp disagrees with this proposition that BLS economies are too small for South Africa to gain substantially from interacting with them. He estimates that over the period 1970–79 exports to BLS contributed 20 per cent of the increase in South African's manufacturing output and 11.3 per cent of the increase in overall gross domestic product.
10. G. Maasdorp, (1993) 'The advantages and disadvantages of current regional institutions for integration', in Pauline H. Baker, Alex Boraine and Warren Krafchik (eds), *South Africa and the Word Economy in the 1990s*. (New York: Brookings Institution).
11. Ibid., p. 36.
12. G. Maasdorp, (1992) 'Trade', in G. Maasdorp and A. Whiteside (eds), *Rethinking Economic Cooperation in Southern Africa: Trade and Investment*. Occasional Papers, Konrad Adenauer Stiftung, Johannesburg.
13. COMESA (1992) Annual Report of the Council of Ministers, Zambia. Press release.
14. PTA, Treaty for the Establishment of the Preferential Trade Area for Eastern and Southern Africa, Lusaka, 1981, pp. 1–2.
15. Ibid., p. 23.
16. PTA, Report of the Second Meeting of PTA Minister of Industry, Nairobi, September 1990, p. 12.

17. Ibid., p. 24.
18. Ibid., p. 25.
19. COMESA, *The State of the Region Nairobi.* Internal Report 1998, p. 6.
20. Ibid., p. 3.
21. PTA, Economic Development in the PTA Area. Internal United Nations Development Report on PTA. UNDU Occasional Paper 5, 1996, p. 5.
22. Ibid., p. 12.
23. Ibid., p. 23.
24. Ibid.
25. Ibid., p. 24.
26. COMESA (2000) Progress Report on Trade, Kenya. P5. Press release 002.
27. IMF (1996) *PTA Economies in Crisis*, IMF Special Report, Issue 14, p. 4 (Internal paper).
28. Ibid., p. 41.
29. Ibid., p. 13.
30. Ibid.
31. Erich Leistner (1992) 'SADCC into SADC: what does it mean?', *South African Foundation Review* (Johannesburg), vol. 18, p. 8.
32. J. Haarlov (1988) *Regional Co-operation in Southern Africa: Central Elements of the SADCC Venture* (Copenhagen: J. Hanlon (1989) *SADCC in the 1990s: Development on the Frontline* (Economist Intelligence Unit) p. 135.
33. Morna (1990a), p. 49.
34. SADCC Annual Progress Report 1991–92.
35. Ibid., p. 24.
36. Quoted in D. Stoneman and C. B. Thompson (1991) *Southern Africa after Apartheid: Economic Repercussions of a Free South Africa*, Africa Recovery Briefing Paper No. 4 (New York: United Nations Department of Public Information), p. 6.
37. SADCC Annual Progress Report 1991–92.
38. *Africa Research Bulletin* (Economic), November/December 1990, p. 10177.
39. The nature of the question was heavily indebted to a 1993 study conducted by Gavin Maasdorp and Alan Whiteside in which a similar study was undertaken to ascertain the views of firms involved in cross-border trade. For a variety of reasons there was a large number of firms who failed to respond to the original questionnaires. As a result, generalizations based on the original study became very difficult. Conversely, the current response has achieved a higher proportional response rate (see G. Maasdorp and Alan Whiteside (1993) *Rethinking Economic Co-operation in Southern Africa: Trade and Investment.* Occasional Papers, Konrad Adenauer Stiftung, Johannesburg).

Chapter 5   Rethinking Regional Security in Southern Africa

1. M. Ayoob (1994) 'The international security system and the Third World' in W. C. Olsen (ed.), *Theory and Practice of International Relations* (Atlantic Highlands, NJ: Prentice Hall) p. 225.

2. Keith Krause and Michael Williams (1997) 'From strategy to security: foundations of critical security studies', in *Critical Security Studies: Concepts and Cases* (London: UCL Press) p. 43
3. Nana Poku and David T. Graham (eds) (1998) *Redefining Security: Population Movements and National Security* (Westport, Conn.: Praeger Publishers).
4. Although what follows assumes a unitary school, realism must be understood less as a coherent theoretical position in its own right than as the site of a great many contested claims and metaphysical disputes. Whether situated against the early twentieth-century crisis of historicism or analysed as yet another benighted footnote to dualism inherited from classical Greek philosophy, claims to political realism in the theory of international relations carry meanings and implications from a much broader discourse about politics and philosophy. Contrary to the assertion of some critics, however, modern realists share, rather than reject, the core premises of their classical predecessors (Ashley, 1984). Indeed, the modern form of realism reiterates the traditional argument that any serious extension of moral and political community beyond the boundaries of the sovereign state is inconceivable in the context of anarchy. It is from these shared values that we can begin to draw some general conclusions about the core assumptions of the realist school. These are: the state, anarchy of the international system, power and security (see Doyle, 1990; Rosenberg, 1990).
5. G. W. F. Hegel (1953) *Reason in History: A General Introduction to the Philosophy of History* (New York: Bobbs Merrill); T. Hobbes (1964) *Leviathan* (New York: Washington Square Press).
6. K. Waltz (1979) *Theory of International Politics* (New York: Random House).
7. F. von Bernhardi (1914) *Germany and the Next War* (New York: Longmans, Green & Co.).
8. Carl von Clausewitz (1976) *On War* (Princeton, NJ: Princeton University Press).
9. C. S. Gray (1988) *The Geopolitics of Super Power* (Lexington: University Press of Kentucky).
10. A. Wolfers (1962) *Discord and Collaboration* (Baltimore, MD: Johns Hopkins University Press).
11. Hans-Georg Gadamer (1983) 'Philosophy or theory of science', in *Reason in the Age of Science*, trans. Frederick G. Lawrence (Cambridge, MA: MIT Press) p. 166.
12. R. Cox (1983) 'Gramsci, hegemony and international relations: an essay in method', *Millennium*, vol. 12, pp. 162–75.
13. B. Barnes (1982) *T. S. Kuhn and Social Science* (London: Macmillan) p. 21.
14. Ibid., p. 25.
15. This is a criterion that I would like to add to the generally accepted three criteria given above. In what follows, we need to draw on all four of the above criteria.
16. House of Assembly Debate, 7 February 1978, col. 579. In many ways the apartheid state sought to reconstruct the African majority so that African

workers could be treated as *Gastarbeiten*, similar in essence to *Gastarbeiten* in Germany and elsewhere in the western world. This is certainly how Verwoerd sought to idealize the black workers in the white state. As David Walsh alleged, they were to remain nationals of their countries of origin (their countries of origin being the Homelands) and they were to work as migrants who obtained no citizen rights within the state in which they worked, p. 156, in Malan to De Klerk.

17. One can observe how, during the cold war, the state sought to legitimate itself to its white constituency (as well as to the western powers) as a key guardian of liberal freedom in the southern African region. Thus, for example, particularly in terms of its intervention in the war in Angola on the side of UNITA, it legitimated its actions abroad by arguing that it was fighting for liberal (Christian) values and against the diabolical illiberal otherness of the Angolan 'communist' (i.e. the MPLA) though of course this legitimation was also projected as an ideal which was commensurable with the state's efforts to preserve a cordon sanitaire between it and the rest of the African continent, a cordon which had all but broken in the aftermath of the decolonization of Rhodesia and the wars of independence in Angola and Mozambique in the 1970s (cf. Arnold, 1992).

18. A. Linklater (1990a) *Beyond Realism and Marxism: Critical Theory and International Relations* (London: Macmillan).

19. A. Linklater (1990b) 'New directions in international relations theory', in H. V. Emy and A. Linklater (eds), *New Horizons in Politics: Essays with an Australian Focus* (Sydney: Allen & Unwin). (Also published as 'The problem of community in international relations', *Alternatives*, vol. XV, pp. 135–53.)

20. M. Mann (1986b) *The Sources of Social Power: the History of Power from the Beginning to 1760 AD*, Vol. 1 (Cambridge: Cambridge University Press).

21. O. Waever (1993) *Securitization and Desecuritization*, Working Paper No. 5 (Copenhagen: Centre for Peace and Conflict Research) pp. 20–1.

22. N. Poku and David Graham (eds) (forthcoming) *Human Security and Migration* (London: Routledge).

23. *UNDP Human Development Report 1994* (Oxford: Oxford University Press, 1994) pp. 4 and 23.

24. *Our Global Neighbourhood: The Commission on Global Governance* (Oxford: Oxford University Press, 1995) p. 84.

25. M. Brown (1996) 'Aid moves from the messianic to the managerial', *The World Today*, June, p. 158.

26. UNDP (1998) *Human Development Report 1994* (New York: Oxford University Press).

27. Statements based on Human Development Indicators, table 2, ibid., pp. 132–3.

28. Ibid.

29. Ibid., table 18, p. 165.

30. Ibid., table 11, p. 151.

31. Ibid.

32. Ibid., table 21, p. 171.
33. D. Gillies (1996) 'Human rights, democracy and good governance: stretching the World Bank's policy frontiers', in J. M. Griesgraber and B. G. Gunter (eds), *The World Bank* (London: Pluto) pp. 101–41 at 101–2.
34. S. P. Riley and T. W. Parfitt (1994) 'Economic adjustment and democratization in Africa', in John Walton and David Seddon (eds), *Free Markets and Food Riots: the Politics of Global Adjustment* (Oxford: Blackwell) pp. 135–70 at p. 140.
35. Ibid., p. 140.
36. UNDP, *Human Development Report*, 1994, op. cit., p. 27.
37. Ibid., p. 28.
38. M. Chossudovsky, cited in *Third World Resurgence*, no. 74, October 1996, p. 17.
39. G. Bird and T. Killick (1995) *The Bretton Woods Institutions: A Commonwealth Perspective* (London: Commonwealth Secretariat) p. 34.
40. *Social Dimensions of Adjustment: World Bank Experience 1980–93* (Washington DC: World Bank) p. 110.
41. UNAIDS (1999a) *Prevention of HIV transmission from mother to child: Strategic options.* Geneva, May.
42. UNAIDS (1998) *AIDS Epidemic Update.* Geneva, December.
43. Ibid.
44. UNAIDS (1998) *Early Data from Mother-to-Child Transmission Study in Africa Finds Shortest Effective Regimen Ever.* Press release, Geneva, February.
45. Josef Decosas and Alix Adrien (1999) *Preliminary Discussion Draft.* Background Paper on HIV Programming in Africa for the Canadian International Development Agency.
46. UNAIDS (1998a) AIDS Epidemic update, December, Annex 2.
47. Daphne Topouzis (1998) *The Implications of HIV/AIDS for Rural Development Policy and Programming: Focus on Sub-Saharan Africa.* Sustainable Development Department, Food and Agriculture Organization, Rome.
48. World Bank (1999) *Population and the World Bank: Adapting to Change* (Washington, DC: World Bank).
49. UNAIDS (1998d) *New Initiative to Reduce HIV Transmission from Mother to Child in Low-Income Countries.* Press release, Geneva, 29 June.
50. World Bank (1997) *Confronting AIDS: Public Priorities in a Global Epidemic* (New York: Oxford University Press).
51. The Policy Project (1999) *The Economic Impact of AIDS* (Draft). The Futures Group International.
52. Topouzis, op. cit.
53. World Bank (1997), op. cit.
54. UNAIDS (1998) *Draft Report on Health Reform and HIV Workshop.* Geneva, 24–26 June.

Select Bibliography

Apter, D. (1996) *Rethinking Development: Modernization, Dependency, and Post-modern Politics*. London: Sage.

Arnold, G. (1992) *South Africa – Crossing the Rubicon*. New York: St. Martin's Press.

Ashley, R. K. (1981) 'Political Realism and Human Interests', *International Studies Quarterly* 25, 2: 204–36.

Ashley, R. K. (1986) 'The Poverty of Neo-Realism' in R. Keohane (ed.) *Neo-Realism and Its Critics*. New York: Columbia University Press.

Axelson, E. (1967) *Portugal and the Scramble for Africa*. Johannesburg: Wits University Press.

Balassa, B. (1961) *The Theory of Economic Integration*. Homewood, IL: Irwin.

Balassa, B. (1966) 'Towards a theory of economic integration', in M. S. Wionczek (ed.), *Latin-American Economic Integration Experience and Prospects*. New York:

Barber, J. (1973) *South Africa's Foreign Policy 1945–1970*. Oxford University Press.

Barber, J. and Barratt, J. (1990) *South Africa's Foreign Policy: The Search for Status and Security*. Johannesburg: Southern.

Beitz, C. (1979) *Political Theory and International Relations*. Princeton, NJ: Princeton University Press.

Bernstein, R. (1983) *Beyond Relativism and Objectivism: Science, Hermeneutics and Praxis*. Oxford: Basil Blackwell.

Blumenfeld, J. (1991) *Economic Interdependence in Southern Africa: From Conflict to Co-operation*. New York: St. Martin's Press.

Brink, A. (1996) *Reinventing a Continent*. Secker & Warburg.

Cecchini, P. (1988) *1992: The Benefits of a Single Market*. Aldershot: Wildwood House.

Chazan, N. (1988) 'State and Society in Africa: images and challenges', in D. Rothchild and N. Chazan (eds), *Precarious Balance: State and Society in Africa*. Boulder, CO: Westview Press.

Cockram, G. M. (1970) *Vorster's Foreign Policy*. Pretoria: Academia.

Cohen, S. B. (1991) 'The emerging world map', in N. Kliot and S. Waterman (ed.), *The Political Geography of Conflict and Peace*. London: Belhaven Press.

Commonwealth Committee of Foreign Ministers on Southern Africa (1989) *South Africa: The Sanctions Report*. London: Penguin.

Cox R. (1987) *Power, Production and World Order*. New York: Colombia University Press.

Craven J. (1990) *An Introduction to Economics*. London: Blackwell.

Davenport, T. R. H. (1991) *South Africa: A Modern History*. London: Macmillan.

Davies, R. and Martin, G. M. (1992) 'Regional prospects and projects: what future for Southern Africa', in S. Vieira, W. G. Martin and I. Wallerstien (eds), *How Fast the Wind? Southern Africa, 1975–2000*. Trenton, NJ: Africa World Press.

Davies, R. H., O'Meara, D. and Dlamini, S. (1985) *The Kingdom of Swaziland*. Tokawa, NJ: Zed Books.

Doyle, M. W. (1990) 'Thucydidean Realism', *Review of International Studies*, 16(3).

Dunner, J. (ed.) (1964) *Dictionary of Political Science*. New York: Philosophical Library.

Escobar, A. (1995) *Encountering Development* (Princeton, NJ: Princeton Univeristy Press).

Evans, P., Rueschemeyer, D. and Skocpol, T. (eds) (1985) *Bringing the State Back In*. New York: Cambridge University Press.

Faure, M. and Land, Jan-Erik (eds) (1996) *South Africa: Designing New Political Institutions*. Sage Publications.

Feld, W. J. and Boyd, G. (eds) (1980) *Comparative Regional Systems*. New York.

Giddens, A. (1984) *The Constitution of Society: Outline of a Theory of Structuration*. Oxford: Polity Press.

Giddens, A. (1985) 'The nation-state and violence', Volume 2 of *A Contemporary Critique of Historical Materialism*. Oxford: Polity Press.

Giddens, A. (1989) 'A reply to my critics', in D. Held and J. Thompson (eds), *Social Theory of Modern Societies: Anthony Giddens and His Critics*. Cambridge: Cambridge University Press.

Geldenhuys, D. J. (1977) 'The effects of South Africa's racial policy on Anglo-South African relations 1945–1961. Unpublished PhD dissertation.

Gertzel, C., et al. (eds) (1984) *The Dynamics of One-Party State in Zambia*. Manchester: Manchester University Press.

Gilpin, R. (1987) *The Political Economy of International Relations*. Princeton, NJ: Princeton University Press.

Girling, J. (1987) *Capital and Power: Social Transformation and Political Economy*. London: Croom Helm.

Goldstein, J. (1988) 'Ideas, institutions and American trade policy', in G. J. Ikenberry et al. (eds), *The State and American Foreign Economic Policy*. Ithaca, NY: Cornell University Press.

Gourevitch, P. (1986) *The Politics of Hard Times: Comparative Responses to International Economic Crises*. Ithaca, NY: Cornell University Press.

Green, R. (1990) 'Economic integration/coordination in Africa: the dream lives but how can it be lived', in J. Pickett and H. Singer (eds), *Towards Economic Recovery in sub-Saharan Africa*. London: Routledge.

Green, R. H. (1981) 'Economic co-ordination, liberation and development: Botswana–Namibia perspectives', in C. Harvey (ed.), *Papers on the Economy of Botswana*. London: Heinemann.

Haarlov, J. (1988) *Regional co-operation in Southern Africa: Central Elements of the SADCC Venture*. Copenhagen: Centre for Development Research.

Haas, E. (1964) *Beyond the Nation State*. Stanford, CA: Stanford University Press.

Haas, E. (1964) 'Technocracy, pluralism and the New Europe', in Stephen Graubard (ed.), *A New Europe?* Boston, MD: Houghton Mifflin.

Haggard, S. (1990) *Pathway from the Periphery*. Ithaca, NY: Cornell University Press.

Hall, J. (1987) *Liberalism: Politics, Ideology and the Market*. London: Paladin-Grafton.

Hamilton, R. and Whalley, J. (1992) *The Future of the World Discrimination Systems*. Washington, DC: Institute for International Economics.

Hanlon, J. (1985) *Beggar Your Neighbour: Apartheid Power in Southern Africa*. London: CIIR.

Hanlon, J. (1986) *Apartheid's Second Front: South Africa's War Against its Neighbours*. London: Penguin.

Hanlon, J. (1989) *SADCC in the 1990s: Development on the Frontline*. London: Economist Intelligence Unit.

Heller, A. (1988) 'The Moral Situation in Modernity', *Social Reserach* 55: 531–50.

Henderson, W. O. (1962) *Studies in German Colonial History*. London: Frank Cass.

Hyam, R. (1972) *The Failure of South Africa's Expansion, 1908–1948*. London: Macmillan.

Jacobson, K. H. and Sidjanski, D. (1980) 'Regional patterns of economic cooperation', in W. J. Feld and G. Boyd (eds), *Comparative Regional Systems*. New York:

Jaster, R. (1988) *The Defence of White Power. South African Foreign Policy under Pressure*. London: Macmillan.

Jones, R. B. J. et al. (1984) *Interdependence on Trial: Studies in the Theory and Reality of Contemporary Interdependence*. London: Pinter.

Katenstein, P. (1985) *Small States in World Markets*. Ithaca, NY: Cornell University Press.

Kaplinsky, R. (1989) *Sanctions Against South Africa*, Report prepared for United Nations Centre on Transnational Corperations. New York: UNCTC.

Keohane, R. (1984) *After Hegemony. Co-operation and Discord in the World Political Economy*. Princeton, NJ: Princeton University Press.

Keohane, R. (1985) 'The world political economy and the crisis of embedded liberalism', in J. Goldthorpe (ed.), *Order and Conflict in Contemporary Capitalism*. Oxford: Clarendon Press.

Keohane, R. (1986) 'The theory of world politics: structural realism and beyond', in R. Keohane (ed.), *Neo-Realism and Its Critics*. New York: Columbia University Press.

Keohane, R. (1988) 'International institutions: two approaches', *International Studies Quarterly*, vol. 32, pp. 376–96.

Keohane, R. (1989) *International Institutions and State Power: Essays in International Relations Theory*. Boulder, CO: Westview Press.

Kindleberger, C. (1973) *American Business Abroad*. New Haven, CT: Yale University Press.

Krauthammer, C. (1992) 'The unipolar moment' in Graham Allison and Gregory Treverton (eds), *Rethinking America's Security: Beyond the Cold War to a New World Order*. New York: W. W. Norton.

Labuschagne, G. S. (1969) *Suid-Afrika en Afrika: Die staatkundige verhouding in die tydperk 1945–1966*. Sentrum vir Internasionle Polititie.

Legum, C. (1976) *Vorster's Gamble for Africa: How the Search for Peace Failed*. London: Rex Collings.

Legum, C. (1988) *The Battlefront of Southern Africa*. New York: Africana.

Lewis, S. R. (1987) *Economics and Apartheid: The Impact of South Africa's Economic Policies*. Institute of Development Studies, University of Sussex.

Libby, T. R. (1987) *The Politics of Economic Power in Southern Africa*. Princeton, NJ: Princeton University Press.

Lindberg, Leon and Scheingold, Stuart (eds) (1971) *Regional Integration: Theory and Research*. Cambridge, MA: Harvard University Press.

Lipietz, A. (1987) *Mirages and Miracles*. London: Verso Press.

Lombard, J. A. (1978) *Freedom, Welfare and Order*. Pretoria: Benbo.

Maasdorp, G. (1982) 'The Southern African Customs Union – an assessment', *Journal of Contemporary African Studies*, vol. 2.

Maasdorp, G. (1990) 'The role of the South African economy, SACU, CMA, and other regional economic groupings'. Unpublished paper delivered at conference: Rethinking Strategies for Mozambique and Southern Africa, Maputo, Mozambique, May 1990.

Maasdorp, G. and Whiteside, A. (1992) *Rethinking Economic Cooperation in Southern Africa: Trade and Investment*. Occasional Paper, Konrad Adenauer Stiftung, Johannesburg.

Maasdorp, G. and Whiteside, A. (eds) (1992) *Towards a Post-Apartheid Future: Political and Economic Relations in Southern Africa*.

Maasdorp, G. and Whiteside, A. (1993) *Rethinking Economic Cooperation in Southern Africa: Trade and Investment*. Occasional Paper, Konrad-Adenauer-Stiftung, Johannesburg.

Maasdorp, G., Robson, P. and Hudson, D. (1995) *Swaziland in the Southern African Customs Union*. A study financed by the European Development Fund for the Government of Swaziland, Capricorn Africa Economic Associates, Mbabane.

McFarland, Earl A. Jr (1983) 'The benefits to the RSA of her export to the BLS countries', in M. A. Oommen et al. (eds), *Botswana's Economy since Independence*. New Delhi: Tata McGraw-Hill.

MacIver, R. M. and Page, C. H. (1955) *Society*. London: Macmillan.

McMillan, J. (1989) 'A game-theoretic view of international trade negotiations: implications for developing countries', in J. Whalley (ed.), *Developing countries and the Global Trading System*. London: Macmillan.

Mandaza, I. (1987) 'Perspectives on economic cooperation and autonomous development in Southern Africa', in S. Amin et al. (eds), *SADCC: Prospects for Disengagement and Development in Southern Africa*. London: Zed Books.

Mandaza, I. (1990) 'SADCC: problems of regional political and economic cooperation in Southern Africa: an overview', cited in A. Nyonyo (ed.), *Regional Integration in Africa. Unfinished Agenda*.

Mann, M. (1986) *The Sources of Social Power: the History of Power from the Beginning to 1760 AD*, vol. 1, Cambridge: Cambridge University Press.

Martin, D. et al. (1986) 'Mozambique: to Nkomati and beyond', in P. Johnson, et al. (eds), *Destructive Engagement: Southern Africa at War*. Harare: Zimbabwe Publishing House.

Martin, D. et al. (1986) 'Zimbabwe: apartheid's dilemma', in P. Johnson et al. (eds), *Destructive Engagement: Southern Africa at War*. Harare: Zimbabwe Publishing House.

Masao, Miyoshi (1994) 'Sites of resistance in the global economy: the case of Southern Africa'. Unpublished paper presented at conference: The Changing Nature of International Political Economy, LSE.

Miller, J. D. B. (1981) *The World of States*. London: Croom Helm.

Minter, W. (1986) *King Solomon's Mines Revisited: Western Interests and the Burdened History of Southern Africa*. Zed Books.

Minter, W. (1994) *Apartheid's Contras: An Inquiry into the Roots of the War in Angola and Mozambique*. Zed Books.

Myrdal, G. (1961) *An International Economy*. New York: Macmillan.

Nathan, L. (1994) *The Changing of the Guard: Armed Forces and Defence Policy in a Democratic South Africa*. Pretoria: HSRC/RGN Publishers.

Nolutshungu, S. C. (1975) *South Africa in Africa*. Manchester: Manchester University Press.

Oden, Bertil (ed.) (1993) *Southern Africa after Apartheid*. Nordiska Afrikainstitut.

Okolo, J. E. and Wright, S. (eds) (1990) *West African Regional Cooperation and Development*. Boulder, Colo. and Oxford: Westview Press.

Ostergaard, T. (1993) 'Classical models of regional integration – what relevance for Southern Africa', in Bertil Oden (ed.), *Southern Africa after Apartheid*.

Parker, G. (1985) *Western Geopolitical Thought in the Twentieth Century*. London: Croom Helm.

Plano, J. C. and Olton, R. (1969) *The International Relations Dictionary*. Holt, Rinehart.

Poku, Nana and Graham, David T. (eds) (1998) *Redefining Security: Population Movements and National Security*. Praeger.

Poku, Nana and Graham, David T. (eds) (1999) *Migration, Globalisation and Human Security*. London: Routledge.

Poku, Nana and Pettiford, Lloyd (eds) (1998) *Redefining the Third World*. London: Macmillan.

PTA (1989) *Study on the Rationalisation and Harmonisation of the Programme Activities of the Intergovernmental Organisations in the PTA Sub-region*. Nairobi.

PTA (1990) *Report on the Ministerial Task Force in Agriculture*. Nairobi.

PTA (1990) *Report of the Second Meeting of PTA Ministers of Industry*. Nairobi.

PTA (1990) *Report of the Twelfth Meeting of the Customs and Trade Committee*. Nairobi.

PTA (1994) *Executive Summery of the Sixteenth Meeting of the Council of Ministers*. Mbabane.

PTA (1995) *Report to the Ninth Meeting of the PTA Authority*. Mbabane.

Ravenhill, D. (ed.) (1986) *Africa in Economic Crisis*. London: Macmillan.

Reading, H. F. (1977) *A Dictionary of Social Science*. London: Routledge.

Reinhardt, R. (1984) 'Historical setting', in H. Nelson (ed.), *Mozambique: A Country Study*. Washington, DC: American University.

Robson, P. (1968) *Economic Integration in Africa*. London: George Allen & Unwin.

Rosenberg, J. (1994) *Empire of Civil Society: A Critique of the Realist Theory of International Relations*. London: Verso.

SADCC (1980) *Southern Africa: Towards Economic Liberation – A Declaration by the Governments of Independent States of Southern Africa*. Lusaka.

SADCC (1981) *Memorandum of Understanding on the Institutionalisation of the Southern African Development Coordination Conference*. Salisbury.

SADCC (1983) *SADCC – Maseru: The Proceedings of the Southern African Development Coordination Conference*. Maseru.

SADCC (1986) *Macro-Economic Survey*. Gaborone, Botswana.

SADCC (1989) *Annual Progress Report*, July.

SADCC (1991) *Towards Economic Integration*, SADCC Internal Working Document. Gaborone, SADCC/SCO/4/91/4.

SADCC (1989) *SADCC Regional Economic Survey 1988*. Gaborone.

SADCC (1989) *SADCC Industrial Development Strategy*. Garborone.

SADCC (1992) *Declaration towards the Southern African Development Community*. Gaborone, Botswana.

SADCC (1992) *SADCC: Towards Economic Integration*, Theme Document for the Annual Consultative Conference (Maputo, 29–31 January).

SADCC (1992) *Towards the Southern African Development Community*. Draft Declaration, SADCC internal working document, March.

Sesay, A. (1990) 'Obstacles to intra-union trade in the Mano River Union', in J. E. Okolo and S. Wright (eds), *West African Regional Cooperation and Development*. Oxford: Westview Press.

Shaw, T. M. (1980) 'Africa', in W. J. Feld and G. Boyd (eds), *Comparative Regional Systems*. New York.

Smuts, J. C. Jr (1952) *Jan Smuts*. London: Cassell.

Stamp, Maxwell (1994) *Namibia: Trade Policy Reform Study: Phase I*. Report prepared for the Ministry of Trade and Industry on behalf of the African Development Fund.

Stoneman, D. and Thompson, C. B. (1991) *Southern Africa after Apartheid: Economic Repercussions of a Free South Africa*, Africa Recovery Briefing Paper No. 4. New York: United Nations Department of Public Information.

Strange, S. (1988) *States and Markets: An Introduction to International Political Economy*. London: Pinter.

Swatuk, L. and Black, D. (eds) (1997) *Bridging the Rift: The New South Africa in Africa*. Boulder, CO: Westview Press.

Taylor, P. (1982) *The State in the European Community in the 1970s: The Limits of International Integration*. PhD thesis, University of London.

Tostenson, A. (1993) 'What role for SADC(C) in the post-apartheid era?', in Bertil Oden (ed.), *Southern Africa After Apartheid*. Nordiska Afrikainstitutet.

UNCTAD (1971) *Trade Extension and Economic Integration Among Developing Countries*. TD/B/85, New York.

Vale, P. (1996) 'Prospects for transplanting European models of regional integration to southern Africa', *Politikon: South African Journal of Political Science*, vol. 9, no. 2, pp. 31–42.

Vale, P. (1993) 'Southern Africa's security: something old, something new', *South African Defence Review*, vol. 9, pp. 33–41.

Valigy, I. and Dora, H. (1992) 'The creation of SADCC and the problems of transport', in Vieira, S. et al. (eds), *How Fast the Wind? Southern Africa 1975–2000*. Trenton, NJ: Africa World Press.

Verwoerd, H. F. (undated) *On Crisis in World Conscience II. The Road to Freedom for Basutoland, Bechuanaland, Swaziland*. Fact Paper 106.

Vieira, S., Martin. W. G. and Wallerstein, I. (eds) (1992) *How Fast the Wind? Southern Africa, 1975–2000*. Trenton, NJ: Africa World Press.

Viner, J. (1950) *The Customs Union Issue*. New York.

Walker, E. A. (1959) *A History of Southern Africa*. London: Longman.

Walker, R. B. J. (1989) 'History and Method in International Relations', *Millennium* 18: 163–83.

Wallerstein, I. (1991) *Geopolitics and Geoculture – Essays on the Changing World System*. Cambridge: Cambridge University Press.

Walter, A. (1983) *World Power and World Money*. Brighton: Harvester Wheatsheaf.

Waltz, K. (1979) *A Theory of International Relations*. Reading, MA: Prentice Hall.

Waltz, K. (1986), 'Reflections on theory of international politics: a response to my critics', in R. Keohane (ed.), *Neo-Realism and Its Critics*. New York: Columbia University Press.

Weimer, B. and Hanlon, J. (1989) *SADCC into the 1990s: Development on the Frontline*. London: Economist Intelligence Unit.

Welch, C. E. Jr (1990) 'The military factor in West Africa: leadership and regional development', in J. E. Okolo and S. Wright (eds), *West African Regional Cooperation and Development*. Oxford: Westview Press.

Wise, M. and Gibb, R. A. (1992) *Single Market to Social Europe: The European Community in the 1990s*. London: Longman.

World Bank (various) *World Development Reports 1989–1994*. Washington DC: World Bank.

World Bank (1991) *Sub-Saharan Africa: From Crisis to Sustainable Growth*. Washington, DC: World Bank.

World Bank (1995) *World Tables 1995*. Washington DC: World Bank.

World Bank (1995) *The World Bank Atlas*. Washington DC: World Bank.

World Bank (1996) *African Development Indicators 1994–95*. Washington DC: World Bank.

World Bank (1996) *Global Economic Prospects*. Washington, DC: World Bank.

World Bank (1997) *International Trade Division Research Summary*. Washington, DC: World Bank.

Zolberg, A. R. (1983) '"World" and "system", a misalliance', in W. R. Thompson (ed.), *Contending Approaches to World Systems Analysis*. Beverly Hills, CA: Sage.

Index